AIR TRAVEL TICKETING
AND
FARE CONSTRUCTION

AIR TRAVEL TICKETING AND FARE CONSTRUCTION

A.P. RASTOGI

Director
J.P. Institute of Hotel Management and Catering Technology
Meerut (Uttar Pradesh)

AMAN PUBLICATIONS
NEW DELHI

ɔlished by
iv Jain for Aman Publications
·4A, Ganpati Bhawan,
'5-B/21, Ansari Road,
ya Ganj, Delhi - 110002
: 23255012, 23282127
ɔail: sshjbs@yahoo.com

ɔt Published 2016

N–81–8204–037–X
'ublisher

ɔE DISTRIBUTOR
JINDAL BOOK SERVICES
LG-4A, Ganpati Bhawan,
4675-B/21, Ansari Road,
Darya Ganj, Delhi - 110002

Jacket Designed by :
S.M. Graphics

Printed at Balaji Offset, India

PREFACE

Airlines provide scheduled air transport services to passengers or freight or chartered flight. They assign prices to their services in an attempt to maximise profitability. To do this well requires yield management technology and pricing flexibility. They use differentiated pricing, a form of price discrimination, in order to sell air services at varying prices simultaneously to different segments. Factors influencing the price include the days remaining until departure, the current booked load factor, the forecast of total demand by price point, competitive pricing in force, and variations by day of week of departure and by time of day.

The advent of advanced computerised reservations systems in the late 1970s, allowed airlines to easily perform cost-benefit analyses on different pricing structures, leading to almost perfect price discrimination in some cases. The intense nature of airfare pricing has led to the term "fare war" to describe efforts by airlines to undercut other airlines on competitive routes. Computers also allow airlines to predict, with some accuracy, how many passengers will actually fly after making a reservation to fly. This allows airlines to overbook their flights enough to fill the aircraft while accounting for "no-shows," but not enough to force paying passengers off the aircraft for lack of seats. Since an average of 1/3 of all seats are flown empty, stimulative pricing for low demand flights coupled with overbooking on high demand flights can help reduce this figure.

Trying to understand all the different fares offered by the nation's airlines is a daunting task. That's because the major carriers have created fare schedules every bit as complex as the federal tax code. So many different fares are available it's unlikely that any two passengers on a given flight will pay the same price for their tickets. Airlines determine fare pricing based on a number of factors, such as the number of seats in each fare category, reservation time periods, competitor pricing on similar flights, and the type of consumers using a particular flight. Computer-assisted revenue management systems are used to examine historical demand to establish the number of seats made available for sale at various fares. Analysts then monitor each flight to adjust seat allocations and fares accordingly.

This book elaborately discusses the principles and procedures of air travel ticketing and fare construction. Its' contents will be highly beneficial to travel agents, tour operators, airline professionals, businessmen, travellers and general public alike.

Editor

CONTENTS

1

INTRODUCTION TO AIR TRAVEL

Aviation or air transport refers to the activities surrounding human flight and the aircraft industry. Aircraft include fixed-wing aircraft, rotary wing (helicopter/autogyro) types, and ornithopters, as well as lighter-than-air craft such as balloons and airships (also known as dirigibles).

HISTORY OF AVIATION

There are records of early, short-distance glider flights from the 10th and 11th centuries, and possibly earlier human-carrying kites from China, but practical human aviation began on November 21, 1783 with the first untethered human flight in a hot air balloon designed by the Montgolfier brothers. A little over a century later, on December 17, 1903, the Wright brothers flew the first successful powered, heavier-than-air flight, though their aircraft was impractical to fly for more than a short distance, due to control problems. The widespread adoption of ailerons made aircraft much easier to manage, and only a decade later, at the start of World War I, heavier-than-air powered aircraft had become practical for reconnaissance, artillery spotting, and even attacks against ground positions.

Between the wars, aircraft grew larger and more reliable, and began to be used to transport people and cargo. In the 1930s, the Douglas DC-3 was the first airliner that was profitable carrying passengers exclusively, starting the modern era of passenger airline service. By the beginning of World War II, many towns and cities had built airports, and there were a large number of qualified pilots available. The war brought many innovations to aviation, including the first jet aircraft and the first liquid-fueled rockets.

After the war, especially in North America, there was a boom in general aviation, both private and commercial, as thousands of pilots were released from military service and many inexpensive war-surplus transport and training aircraft were available. Small aircraft manufacturers such as Cessna, Piper, and Beechcraft expanded production to provide small aircraft for the new middle class market.

By the 1950s, the development of civil jets grew, beginning with the de Havilland Comet, though the first widely-used passenger jet was the Boeing 707. At the same time, turboprop propulsion began to appear for smaller commuter planes, making it possible to serve small-volume routes in a much wider range of weather conditions.

Yuri Gagarin was the first human to travel to space on April 12, 1961 while the Apollo 11 crew first were the first to set foot on the moon on July 21, 1969.

Since the 1960s, composite airframes and quieter, more efficient engines have become available, but the most important innovations have taken place in instrumentation and control. The arrival of solid-state electronics, the Global Positioning System, satellite communications, and increasingly small and powerful computers and LED displays, have dramatically changed the cockpits of airliners and, increasingly, of smaller aircraft as well. Pilots can navigate much more accurately and view terrain, obstructions, and other nearby aircraft on a map or through synthetic vision, even at night or in low visibility.

On June 21, 2004, SpaceShipOne became the first privately-funded aircraft to make a spaceflight, opening the possibility of an aviation market outside the earth's atmosphere.

CIVIL AVIATION

Civil aviation includes all non-military flying, both general aviation and scheduled air transport. While there were many more in the past, there are currently only five major manufacturers of transport aircraft:

— Boeing, based in the United States

— Airbus, based in Europe

— Bombardier, based in Canada

— Embraer, based in Brazil

— Tupolev, based in Russia

Boeing, Airbus, and Tupolev concentrate on larger airliners, while Bombardier and Embraer concentrate on commuter aircraft.

Until the 1970s, most major airlines were flag carriers, sponsored by their governments and heavily protected from competition. Since then, various open skies agreements have resulted in increased competition and choice for consumers, coupled with falling prices for airlines. The combination of high fuel prices, low fares, high salaries, and crises such as the September 11, 2001 attacks and the SARS epidemic have driven many older airlines to government-bailouts, bankruptcy or mergers. At the same time, low-cost carriers such as Ryanair and Southwest have flourished.

GENERAL AVIATION

General aviation includes any flight that is not military and does not fly on a regular schedule, ranging from a recreational flight in a hang glider to a non-scheduled cargo flight in a Boeing 747. The majority of flights on any day will fall into this category.

Because of the huge range of activities, it is difficult to cover general aviation with a simple description — general aviation may include business flights, private aviation, flight training, parachuting, gliding, air ambulance, crop dusting, charter flights, traffic reporting, police air patrols, forest fire flighting, and many other types of flying.

Each country regulates aviation differently, but typically, general aviation falls under several different types of regulations depending on whether it is private or commercial and on the type of equipment involved.

Many small aircraft manufacturers, including Cessna, Piper, Mooney, Cirrus Design, Raytheon, and others serve the general aviation market, with a focus on private aviation and flight training. The most important recent developments for small aircraft have been the introduction of advanced avionics (including GPS) that were formerly found only in large airliners, and the introduction of composite materials to make small aircraft lighter and faster.

MILITARY AVIATION

The Lockheed SR-71 was remarkably advanced for its time and remains unsurpassed in many areas of performance. Simple airships were used as surveillance aircraft as early as the 18th century. Over the years, military aircraft have been built to meet ever increasing capability requirements. Manufacturers of military aircraft compete for contracts to supply their government's arsenal. Aircraft are selected based on factors like cost, performance, and the speed of production.

AIR TRAFFIC CONTROL (ATC)

Air traffic control (ATC) involves humans (typically on the ground) who communicate with aircraft to help maintain separation — that is, they ensure that aircraft are far enough apart horizontally or vertically that there is no risk of collision. Controllers may co-ordinate position reports provided by pilots, or in high traffic areas (such as the United States) they may use RADAR to see aircraft positions.

While the exact terminology varies from country to country, there are generally three different types of ATC:

— control towers (including tower, ground control, clearance delivery, and other services), which control aircraft within a small distance (typically 10-15 km horizontal, and 1,000 m vertical) of an airport.

— terminal controllers, who control aircraft in a wider area (typically 50-80 km) around busy airports

— centre controllers, who control aircraft enroute between airports

ATC is especially important for aircraft flying under Instrument flight rules (IFR), where they may be in weather conditions that do not allow the pilots to see other aircraft. However, in very high-traffic areas, especially near major airports, aircraft flying under Visual flight rules (VFR) are also required to follow instructions from ATC.In addition to separation from other aircraft, ATC may provide weather advisories, terrain separation, navigation assistance, and other services to pilots, depending on their workload.

It is important to note that ATC does not control all flights. The majority of VFR flights in North America are not required to talk to ATC at all (unless they're passing through a busy terminal area or using a major airport), and in many areas, such as northern Canada, ATC services are not available even for IFR flights at lower altitudes.

AIRLINE

An airline provides scheduled air transport services to passengers or freight or chartered flight. Airlines lease or own their aircraft with which to supply these services and may form partnerships or alliances with other airlines for reasons of mutual benefit.

Airlines vary from those with a single airplane carrying mail or cargo, through full-service international airlines operating many hundreds of airplanes. Airline services can be categorized as being intercontinental, intracontinental, regional or domestic and may be operated as scheduled services or charters.

Patterns

The pattern of ownership has gone from government owned or supported to independent, for-profit public companies. This occurs as regulators permit greater freedom, in steps that are usually decades apart. This pattern has not been completed for all airlines in all regions.

The demand for air travel services depends on: business needs for cargo shipments, business passenger demand, leisure passenger demand, all influenced by economic activity.

The overall trend of demand has been consistently increasing. In the 1950's and 1960's, annual growth rates of 15% or more were common. Annual growth of 5-6%

persisted through the 1980's and 1990's. Growth rates are not consistent in all regions, but certainly areas where deregulation provided more competition and greater pricing freedom resulted in lower fares and sometimes dramatic spurts in traffic growth. The U.S., Australia, Japan, Brazil, Mexico, and other markets exhibited this trend.

The industry is cyclical. Four or five years of poor performance are followed by five or six years of gradually improving good performance. But profitability in the good years is generally low, in the range of 2-3% net profit after interest and tax. It is in this time that airlines begin paying for new generations of airplanes and other service upgrades they ordered to respond to the increased demand. Since 1980, the industry as a whole has not even earned back the cost of capital during the best of times. Conversely, in bad times losses can be dramatically worse.

Warren Buffett once said that despite all the money that has been invested in all airlines, the net profit is less than zero. He believes that it is one of the hardest business to manage.

As in many mature industries, consolidation is a trend, as airlines form new business combinations, ranging from loose, limited bilateral partnerships to long-term, multi-faceted alliances of groups of companies, to equity arrangements between companies, to actual mergers or takeovers. Since governments often restrict ownership and merger between companies in different countries, most consolidation takes place within a country. In the U.S., over 200 airlines have been merged, taken over, or simply gone out of business since deregulation began in 1978. Many international airline managers are lobbying their governments to permit greater consolidation, in order to achieve higher economies of scale and greater efficiencies.

Following World War I, the United States found itself swamped with aviators. Many decided to take their war-surplus aircraft on barnstorming campaigns, performing acrobatic maneuvers to woo crowds. In 1918, the United States Postal Service won the financial backing of Congress to begin experimenting with air mail service, initially using Curtiss Jenny aircraft that had been procured by the United States Army for reconnaissance missions on the Western Front. The Army was the first to fly these missions, but quickly lost the contract when they proved to be too unreliable. By the mid-1920s, the Postal Service had developed its own air mail network, based on a transcontinental backbone between New York and San Francisco. To supplant this service, they offered twelve contracts for spur routes to independent bidders: the carriers that won these routes would, through time and mergers, evolve into Braniff Airways, American Airlines, United Airlines (originally a division of Boeing), Trans World Airlines, Northwest Airlines, and Eastern Air Lines, to name a few.

Passenger service during the early 1920s was sporadic: most airlines at the time were focused on carrying bags of mail. In 1925, however, Ford Motor Company bought out the Stout Aircraft Company and began construction of the all-metal Ford Trimotor, the first successful American airliner. With a 12-passenger capacity, it made passenger service potentially profitable. Air service was seen as a supplement to rail service in the American transportation network.

At the same time, Juan Trippe began a crusade to create an air network that would link America to the world, and he achieved this goal through his airline, Pan American World Airways, with a fleet of flying boats that linked Los Angeles to Shanghai and Boston to London. Pan Am was the only U.S. airline to go international before the 1940s.

With the introduction of the Boeing 247 and Douglas DC-3 in the 1930s, the U.S. airline industry was generally profitable, even during the Great Depression. This trend continued until the beginning of World War II.

EARLY DEVELOPMENT OF AIRLINES IN EUROPE

The first countries in Europe to embrace air transport were Finland, France, Germany and the Netherlands. KLM was founded in 1919, the oldest carrier operating under its original name. The first flight transported two English passengers to Schiphol, Amsterdam from London in 1920. Like other major European airlines of the time, KLM's early growth depended heavily on the needs to service links with far-flung colonial possessions (Dutch Indies). It is only after the loss of the Dutch Empire that KLM found itself based at a small country with few potential passengers, depending heavily on transfer traffic, and was one of the first to introduce the hub-system to facilitate easy connections.

France began an air mail service to Morocco in 1919 that was bought out in 1927, renamed Aéropostale, and injected with capital to become a major international carrier. In 1933, Aéropostale went bankrupt, was nationalized and merged with several other airlines into what became Air France.

In Finland, the charter establishing Aero O/Y (now Finnair, one of the oldest still-operating airlines in the world) was signed in the city of Helsinki on 12th September, 1923. Junkers F 13 D-335 became the first aircraft of the company, when Aero took delivery of it on 14th March, 1924. The first flight was between Helsinki and Tallinn, capital of Estonia, and it took place on 20th March 1924, one week later.

The German airline industry began with Lufthansa in 1926, which, unlike most other airlines at the time, became a major investor in airlines outside of Europe, founding Varig and Avianca. German airliners built by Junkers, Dornier, and Fokker were the most advanced in the world at the time. The peak of German air travel came in the mid-1930s, when Nazi propaganda ministers approved the start of commercial zeppelin service: the big airships were a symbol of industrial might, but the fact that they used flammable hydrogen gas raised safety concerns that culminated with the Hindenburg disaster of 1937.

United Kingdom's flag carrier during this period was Imperial Airways, which became BOAC (British Overseas Airlines Co.) in 1939. Imperial Airways used huge Handley-Page biplanes for routes between London, the Middle East, and India: images of Imperial aircraft in the middle of the Rub'al Khali, being maintained by Bedouins, are among the most famous pictures from the heyday of the British Empire.

DEVELOPMENT OF AIRLINES POST-1945

As governments met to set the standards and scope for an emergent civil air industry toward the end of the war, it was no surprise that the U.S. took a position of maximum operating freedom. After all, U.S. airline companies were not devastated by the war, as European companies and the few Asian companies had been. This preference for "open skies" operating regimes continues, within limitations, to this day.

World War II, like World War I, brought new life to the airline industry. Many airlines in the Allied countries were flush from lease contracts to the military, and foresaw a future explosive demand for civil air transport, for both passengers and cargo. They were eager to invest in the newly emerging flagships of air travel such as the Boeing Stratocruiser, Lockheed Constellation, and Douglas DC-6.

Most of these new aircraft were based on American bombers such as the B-29, which had spearheaded research into new technologies such as pressurization. Most offered increased efficiency from both added speed and greater payload.

In the 1950s, the De Havilland Comet, Boeing 707, Douglas DC-8, and Sud Aviation Caravelle became the first flagships of the Jet Age in the West, while the Soviet Union bloc countered with the Tupolev Tu-104 and Tupolev Tu-124 in the fleets of state-owned carriers such as Aeroflot and Interflug. The Vickers Viscount and Lockheed L-188 Electra inaugurated turboprop transport.

The next big boost for the airlines would come in the 1970s, when the Boeing 747, McDonnell Douglas DC-10, and Lockheed L-1011 inaugurated widebody ("jumbo jet") service, which is still the standard in international travel. The Tupolev Tu-144 and its Western counterpart, Concorde, made supersonic travel a reality. In 1972, Airbus began producing Europe's most commercially successful line of airliners to date. The added efficiencies for these aircraft were often not in speed, but in passenger capacity, payload, and range.

With deregulation in the U.S. beginning in 1978, barriers to entry were lowered for new entrants. Typically, a new wave of start-ups would enter during downturns in the normal 8-10 year business cycle. At that time, they find aircraft, financing, hangar and maintenance services, training all relatively inexpensive, and laid off staff from other companies eager and willing to take a job with the new company.

Alas, as the business cycle returned to normalcy, major airlines were able to dominate their routes through aggressive pricing and additional capacity offerings, often swamping the new startup. Only America West Airlines has remained as a significant survivor from this new entrant era, as dozens, even hundreds, have gone under.

In many ways, the biggest winner in the deregulated environment was the air passenger. Indeed, the U.S. witnessed an explosive growth in demand for air travel, as many millions who had never or rarely flown before became regular fliers, even joining frequent flyer loyalty programs and receiving free flights and other benefits from their flying. New services and higher frequencies meant that business fliers could fly to another city, do business, and return the same day, for almost any points in the country. Air travel's advantages put intercity bus lines under pressure, and most have withered away.

By the 1980's, almost half of the total flying in the world took place in the U.S., and today the domestic industry operates over 10,000 daily departures nationwide.

Toward the end of the century, a new style of low cost airline appeared, offering a product at a price that was well-received. JetBlue, AirTran Airways, and other companies represented a serious challenge to legacy carriers, as their counterparts in Europe, Canada, and Asia did to legacy carriers in those regions. Their commercial viability also represented a serious cost threat to employees at legacy airlines, as they set the standard for wage rates in the industry that were a fraction of the prevailing wage.

Thus the last 50 years of the airline industry have varied from reasonably profitable, to devastatingly depressed. As the first major market to deregulate the industry in 1978, U.S. airlines have experienced more turbulence than almost any other country or region. Today, airlines representing approximately one-half of total U.S. seat capacity are operating under bankruptcy provisions.

REGULATORY CONSIDERATIONS

Many countries have national airlines that are owned and operated by the government. Even fully privatized airlines are subject to a great deal of government regulation for economic, political, and safety concerns. Airline labor actions, for instance, are often halted by government intervention in order to protect the free flow of people, communications, and goods between different regions without compromising safety.

The United States, Australia, and to a lesser extent Brazil, Mexico, the United Kingdom, and Japan have "deregulated" their airlines. In the past, these governments dictated airfares, route networks, and other operational requirements for each airline. Since deregulation, airlines have been largely free to negotiate their own operating arrangements with different airports, enter and exit routes easily, and to levy airfares and supply flights according to market demand.

The entry barriers for new airlines are lower in a deregulated market, and so the U.S. has seen hundreds of airlines start up (sometimes for only a brief operating period). This has produced far greater competition than before deregulation in most markets, and average fares tend to drop 20% or more, spurring new sources of demand. The added competition, together with pricing freedom, means that new entrants often take market share with highly reduced rates that, to a limited degree, full service airlines must match. This is a major constraint on profitability for established carriers, which tend to have a higher cost base.

As a result, profitability in a deregulated market is uneven for most airlines. These forces have caused some major airlines to go out of business, in addition to most of the poorly established new entrants.

International Regulation

Groups such as the International Civil Aviation Organization establish worldwide standards for safety and other vital concerns. Most international air traffic is regulated by bilateral agreements between countries, which designate specific carriers to operate on specific routes. The model of such an agreement was the Bermuda Agreement between the US and UK following World War II, which designated airports to be used for transatlantic flights and gave each government the authority to nominate carriers to operate routes.

Bilateral agreements are based on the "freedoms of the air," a group of generalized traffic rights ranging from the freedom to overfly a country to the freedom to provide domestic flights within a country (a very rarely granted right known as cabotage). Most agreements permit airlines to fly from their home country to designated airports in the other country: some also extend the freedom to provide continuing service to a third country, or to another destination in the other country while carrying passengers from overseas.

In the 1990s, "open skies" agreements became more common, which take many of these regulatory powers from state governments and open up international routes to further competition. Open skies agreements have met some criticism, particularly within the European Union, whose airlines would be at a comparative disadvantage with the United States' because of cabotage restrictions.

ECONOMIC CONSIDERATIONS

Although many countries continue to operate state-owned or parastatal airlines, most large airlines today are privately-owned and are therefore governed by microeconomic principles in order to maximize shareholder profit.

The airline industry as a whole has made a cumulative loss during its 120-year history, once subsidies for aircraft development and airport construction are included in the cost. The lack of profitability and continuing government subsidies are justified with the argument that positive externalities, such as higher growth due to global mobility, outweigh microeconomic losses. A historically high level of government intervention in the airline industry can be seen as part of a wider political consensus on strategic forms of transport, such as highways and railways, both of which are also publicly run in most parts of the world. Profitability is likely to improve in future as privatization continues and more competitive low-cost carriers proliferate.

Financing

Airline financing is quite complex, since airlines are highly leveraged operations. Not only must they purchase (or lease) new airline bodies and engines regularly, they must make major long-term fleet decisions with the goal of meeting the demands of their markets while producing a fleet that is relatively economical to operate and maintain. Compare Southwest Airlines and their reliance on a single airplane type (the Boeing 737 and derivatives), with the now bankrupt Eastern Air Lines which operated 17 different aircraft types, each with varying pilot, engine, maintenance, and support needs.

A second financial issue is that of hedging oil and fuel purchases, usually second only to labor in its relative cost to the company but with the current high fuel prices it has become biggest part of total airlines expenses. While hedging instruments can be expensive, they can easily pay for themselves many times over in periods of increasing fuel costs, such as in the 2000-2005 period.

OPERATING COSTS

Full-service airlines have a high level of fixed and operating costs in order to establish and maintain air services: labor, fuel, airplanes, engines, spares and parts, IT services and networks, airport equipment, airport handling services, sales distribution, catering, training, insurance, and other costs. Thus all but a small percentage of the income from ticket sales is paid out to a wide variety of external providers or internal cost centers.

Moreover, the industry is structured so that airlines often act as tax collectors. Airline fuel is untaxed however due to a series of treaties existing between countries. Ticket prices include a number of fees, taxes, and surcharges they have little or no control over, and these are passed through to various providers. Airlines are also responsible for enforcing government regulations. If airlines carry passengers without proper documentation on an international flight, they are responsible for returning them back to the originating country.

Analysis of the 1992-1996 period shows that every player in the air transport chain is far more profitable than the airlines, who collect and pass through fees and revenues to them from ticket sales. While airlines as a whole earned 6% return on capital employed (2-3.5% less than the cost of capital), airports earned 10%, catering companies 10-13%, handling companies 11-14%, aircraft lessors 15%, aircraft manufacturers 16%, and global distribution companies more than 30%.

In contrast, Southwest Airlines has been the most profitable of airline companies since 1970. Indeed, some sources have calculated Southwest to be the best performing stock over the period, outperforming Microsoft and many other high performing companies. The chief reasons for this are their product consistency and cost control.

The widespread entrance of a new breed of low cost airlines beginning at the turn of the century has accelerated the demand that full service carriers control costs. Many of these low cost companies emulate Southwest Airlines in various respects, and like Southwest, they are able to eke out a consistent profit throughout all phases of the business cycle.

As a result, a shakeout of airlines is occurring in the U.S. and elsewhere. United Airlines, US Airways (twice), Delta Air Lines, and Northwest Airlines have all declared Chapter 11 bankruptcy, and American has barely avoided doing so. Alitalia, Scandinavian Airlines System, SABENA, Japan Air System, Air Canada, Ansett Australia, and others have flirted with or declared bankruptcy since 2000, as low cost entrants enter their home markets as well. Some argue that it would be far better for the industry as a whole if a wave of actual closures were to reduce the number of "undead" airlines competing with healthy airlines while being artificially protected from creditors via bankruptcy law.

2

MODERN TRENDS IN AIR TRANSPORT

Commercial aviation has undergone enormous growth over its relatively short history as the globalisation of industry and commerce has increased and air travel's relative affordability has contributed both to a boom in international tourism and to a large rise in the volume of air freight. Air transport has become an integral part of many people's lifestyle and its continued growth is taken for granted by many.

Various forecasts of growth are available. One of the most widely accepted for the UK is from the Department for Transport, Local Government and the Regions (DTLR),which gives a mid-range scenario prediction that air traffic at UK airports will grow at an average of 4.25% per annum. This is based on 'unconstrained forecasts of the underlying demand for air travel' up to 2030 and is intended to cover all market segments.

The Department's highest and lowest growth scenarios are for growth at 4.9% and 3.6% respectively. Without the restriction of any limiting measures imposed at global, European or national level, these forecasts imply that British airports will be serving over one billion passengers a year by 2050.

'Passenger-kilometres' flown from UK airports increased from 125 billion in 1990 to 260 billion in 2000.The most rapid growth has been seen in international travel, though domestic flights have also risen steadily. The huge expansion of the 'no-frills carriers' has contributed to this growth. In the last five years the passenger-kilometres carried by these operators have more than doubled, and now account for about 20% of the total passenger-kilometres flown from UK airports.This is even more remarkable considering that these services operate only on domestic and short-haul routes.

Until 2001 the actual growth rate followed one of the higher growth scenarios although there was a drop below that trend in 2001 which was accentuated following the terrorist attacks in the USA on 11 September 2001. Many analysts believe this downturn to be temporary, and signs of recovery are already apparent.

The DfT has stated that 'despite fluctuations arising from economic and other events, traffic growth will return to its long run trend'. Largely helped by the rise in express delivery services, which require airports with 24-hour operation, air freight has been growing even faster than passenger transport. The tonnage of freight carried by air, landing or taking off at UK airports, rose by an average of 8.7% per annum between 1992 and 1998 and this trend is expected to continue. In 2001, 18.7% of tonnage of freight landing at or taking off from UK airports was carried between the UK and the other European Union Member States; 2.7% was carried over domestic routes. The majority of air freight though is carried over longer distances.

Originally air freight was used only as a way to fill excess storage space in passenger aircraft, but as wider bodied planes were developed, freight transport became an important activity in its own right. This eventually resulted in all-cargo aircraft. In 2001, a third of air freight landing or taking off from UK airports was carried in all-cargo aircraft.The DfT's consultation on the future development of air transport in the regions includes proposals to establish airports supplying 'substantial, dedicated air freight provision', including the suggestion to develop Alconbury, Cambridgeshire as an 'express parcel hub'.

Although we have limited our attention to commercial aircraft, we note that a significant, if falling, proportion of the world's aircraft is military. In 1992, 18% of the world's fleet were military aircraft and by 2015 they are estimated to amount to 7%.In the early 1990s, military aircraft consumed approximately one third of the fuel used by the commercial fleet.The performance requirements of military aircraft suggest that, compared to civil aircraft, they are likely to produce proportionately more emissions of some climate-changing pollutants, oxides of nitrogen in particular.

SERVICE LIVES OF AIRCRAFT

Some of the environmental impacts of flight can be addressed through new technology. However, there is a considerable delay between the development of conceptual new technologies and such developments becoming available for use.

Evidence to us indicated that a new design for aircraft might take ten years in development and another ten in construction.The aircraft would then be expected to be in service for three decades. Consequently, new technologies will take at least twenty years to come into use and following that there will be a period during which a proportion of older, more polluting stock will remain in service. This 'overlap' problem is compounded by the growth of small carriers and of airline industries in developing countries. Large airlines in developed countries sell on their out-of-date stock to these younger airlines, meaning that such craft can remain in service even longer.

Even so, the gradual replacement of the old aircraft fleet with newer designs ought to have a positive environmental impact. But this must be considered against the fact that new aircraft are not designed primarily for their environmental features, as is apparent in some aircraft designs currently under discussion.

The aviation industry has brought many benefits to society in both economic and social terms. The relative affordability and speed of air transport today have made international travel accessible to many people who would never previously have had the time or financial means to enable them to travel overseas.

This broadening of the collective horizon is likely to benefit society generally, even though the proportion of the global population who are able to travel in this way remains small. The wide availability of air transport is still limited to the affluent developed world and to the elite few in the developing countries. However, the environmental costs of aviation can be global: climate change will affect every person and its consequences may be most damaging for those in the developing world.

One study estimates that the aviation industry directly provides jobs for over 180,000 people in the UK, and contributes some £10.2 billion to the gross domestic product.In addition the Department for Trade and Industry (DTI) draws attention to the trade in goods, industrial developments and economic services that air transport facilitates.This trade creates wealth, which, the DTI believes, could be used for global as well as national development. The extent to which these benefits, in practice, improve global conditions is difficult to ascertain. How much they would be compromised if the growth in aviation were curtailed would depend on the ways in which this was done and the quality of the alternative transport and communication methods available. In any case the resources displaced by restrictions on air transport would find other uses in due course, probably with similar or only slightly lower market value and much less damaging environmentally.

Many different industries are involved in the aviation sector. Separate companies construct engines and airframes; airlines and air freight companies are independent organisations, as are the airports from which they fly; and many other companies supply a range of goods and services. All these organisations are distinct, yet have to co-operate and work closely together.

The industry is subject to air traffic control systems and regulation from bodies such as the Civil Aviation Authority (CAA) in the UK and, at an international level, the International Civil Aviation Organisation (ICAO). ICAO was set up in 1947 and is the permanent body charged with the administration of the principles set out in the 1944 Convention on International Civil Aviation (Chicago Convention) and is a specialised agency of the United Nations (UN). ICAO has 188 contracting states.

ICAO includes in its aims: 'to achieve maximum compatibility between the safe and orderly development of civil aviation and the quality of the environment'.Its current environmental activities are largely undertaken through the Committee on Aviation Environmental Protection (CAEP), which has eighteen members.CAEP comprises five working groups; two focussing on aircraft noise issues, two on emissions and one dealing with market-based measures. It sets out its recommendations every three years for consideration and possible adoption by the ICAO Assembly.

ICAO has no powers of enforcement and sets only recommended standards and guidelines. Its members are bound morally rather than legally to act in accordance with the ICAO resolutions. It is up to individual countries to transfer the standards into national law, and in some cases member states deviate from the recommendations, or do not implement them at all.

AIRFRAME DEVELOPMENT

Currently, the development of airframes is split between serving two market views, 'fragmentation' and 'consolidation'. The fragmentation view is that a larger number of direct flights will occur between 'local' airports so creating a requirement for a large number of smaller, higher speed aircraft. The consolidation view sees further development in 'hub airports', flights between which would be provided by larger high capacity aircraft. Such hubs would be nodes in an integrated transport system, possibly including flights to and from smaller regional 'feeder' airports, a role which might be played by an improved rail or multimodal network.

Over a set distance, smaller aircraft often have lower emissions per flight than larger aircraft, but their emissions per passenger kilometre are greater. The higher altitude at which the newer designs of aircraft might fly could also increase their impact on the climate.

The increasing development of hub airports in the consolidation model also raises problems. It is possible that as aircraft become larger aircraft emissions affecting air quality within the airport boundary might increase at a rate greater than aircraft movements. There may come a point when local air quality issues become the main limiting factor on the growth in the use of these hubs by aircraft.

Over the past 40 years, fuel burn and emissions of carbon dioxide and oxides of nitrogen have reduced dramatically for new aircraft, owing to increased efficiency of airframe and engine design. Improvement is complicated by the competition between developing quieter engines and reducing emissions.

PASSENGER DENSITY

The number of passenger movements is currently increasing faster than the number of aircraft movements because of the development of bigger aircraft with a higher passenger capacity. However, overall, passenger densities are decreasing at present. This is caused by the increase in business and first class travel, which use the increase in space available per passenger as a selling point.

Furthermore, most flights do not fly at full capacity. On average only 78% of seats on international flights, and 65% on domestic flights, are filled. This causes difficulty in interpreting figures for emissions per passenger-kilometre, which are often calculated on the basis of a full aircraft. Measures to increase passenger density might reduce emissions per passenger-kilometre and result in fewer aircraft movements for a given number of passengers. Such measures may simply result in increasing the numbers of passenger movements as airlines would be tempted to maximise profits by not reducing the number of aircraft movements but by filling those flights.

REGULATION AND TAXATION

Unlike fuel for motor vehicles or trains, under an interpretation of Article 24 of the 1944 Chicago Convention, there is no tax levied on fuel for aviation, either as fuel duty or VAT. This interpretation has been implemented through some 4,000 bilateral agreements between nations, making any renegotiation difficult. Exemption from taxation amounts to a subsidy for the aviation industry, compared with most other modes of transport. Shipping is also tax-exempt as no duty is levied on maritime fuel.

Arguments against placing taxes on aircraft fuel rest on the difficulty of securing united global action, while unilateral action would simply result in 'tankering' - fuel being purchased in countries where it was not taxed, and transported to where it was needed - thus aggravating the problem. We are not convinced by such arguments, at least as applying to any EU level initiative, as proposed below. There is a strong case for some form of charging, not least to reflect the 'polluter pays principle'.

The Kyoto Protocol was signed in 1997, committing signatories to cutting emissions of 'greenhouse gases' by 5.2% of 1990 levels by 2012. However, international aviation and maritime emissions were excluded from the Kyoto Protocol under Article 2.2. Responsibility for regulating emissions from international aviation has been left to ICAO, which has no powers of enforcement. Domestic aviation is covered under the Kyoto Protocol and currently accounts for about 0.5% of the UK's carbon dioxide emissions; but the Kyoto Protocol places limits only on carbon dioxide emissions, not the emissions of oxides of nitrogen and water vapour. These gases, when emitted at high altitudes, cause more damage than they do at ground level, resulting in greater 'radiative forcing' from aviation than might be expected from its carbon dioxide emissions alone.

TRENDS OF AIR TRANSPORT IN EUROPE

Aviation is a quintessentially international industry. There are few areas, apart from airport development, in which a country is free to make policy in isolation from other countries. In the European Union (EU), the creation of the single market has dismantled traditional restrictions on market access, capacity, frequencies and fares. Airline licensing, slot allocation, ground handling and various aspects of consumer protection are all subject to Community law. Member States have also been ready to accept that the EU should take the lead in appropriate technical fields such as safety regulation, air traffic management and environmental matters. This has led to the creation of the European Aviation Safety Agency and proposals for a 'Single European Sky' for the purposes of air traffic management.

Over the next 10 years we can expect to see further developments, including extension of the single aviation market to include those states which will have acceded to the EU, and perhaps some neighbouring countries as well; and an increasing role for the EU in conducting aviation relations with other countries. In addition there will be further development of the 'Single European Sky', and a consequent decrease in the number of air traffic management centres in Europe. The European Aviation Safety Agency (EASA) is likely to take on responsibility for rule-making in all matters relating to operations, personnel, airports and air traffic management.

Global standards in such areas as safety, air traffic management, navigation satellite systems, security, and accident investigation will continue to be set by ICAO. This will help to secure stable, harmonised and internationally recognised standards, and avoid a proliferation of local rules.

The International Civil Aviation Organisation (ICAO) is a United Nations Specialist Agency which aims to promote the safe and efficient development of international civil aviation. Founded in 1944, ICAO currently has 188 Contracting States. Contracting States are obliged either to comply with the minimum safety, security and environmental standards established by ICAO, or to inform other States of variations.

ECAC was founded in 1955 to promote co-operation between European states on civil aviation matters. It is not a law-making body, but provides a forum for the exchange of views, advice and information. ECAC currently has 41 Member States, and is particularly active in assisting European countries with less developed aviation industries.

EUROCONTROL (The European Organisation for the Safety of Air Navigation) develops short, medium and long-term initiatives in a collaborative effort with 33 Member States, industry, and airspace users. Since its inception, Eurocontrol has promoted a number of significant benefits to the European air traffic management system, including the setting up of the Central Route Charges Office, which collects and disburses route charges on behalf of Member States.

Safety Issues

Safety will continue to be of prime importance across the aviation sector. The air transport industry has a good record, with accident rates kept low despite the rapid rise in traffic levels over the past two decades. In seeking improvements, there is the importance of independent checks on the national safety systems. Both the CAA and the Department for Transport's Air Accidents Investigation Branch have already been audited by ICAO experts and received good reports. Both organisations will take the necessary remedial action where an audit suggests things can be done better, and will continue to be subject to follow-up checks. In addition, the CAA will ensure that the proper level of safety regulation is delivered as cost-effectively as possible.

Within Europe, a genuinely single market in air transport services calls for common rules and harmonised standards of implementation. Establishing a properly resourced and legally robust regime, based on the EASA, for ensuring high safety standards across Europe is an important step forward. EASA delivers an efficient, high quality safety regime as the European Common Aviation

Area gradually expands. In supporting liberalisation beyond Europe, it will not lead to lower safety standards or loss of effective safety oversight, and must ensure clear lines of responsibility leading back to specifically accountable regulatory authorities.

For people living and working near airports, safety is best assured by ensuring the safe operation of aircraft in flight. However, in areas where accidents are most likely to occur it is importanr to control the number of people at risk through the Public Safety Zone system. Public Safety Zones are areas of land at the ends of runways at the busiest airports, within which development is restricted.

The primary aim of aviation security is the protection of aircraft and their occupants. It is right, for industry to meet the full costs of security - as it does other running costs - and to pass these costs on to the consumer as appropriate. Tod,·y an important vulnerability arises beyond the shores, in countries whose aviation security arrangements may be less robust - in some cases very much less. The aviation ir dustry is changing rapidly. Aviation security evolves ·n parallel, both through improvements to the measures already in place and identification and development of imaginative new approaches and maximum use of new technologies.

Service Quality

Standards of service are a legitimate element of competition between operators. Many travellers, for example, attach more importance to price than to in-flight service, particularly on shorter routes. Healthy competition between operators and reliable consumer information are the starting points for ensuring that the customer gets good value for money.

The steady growth in the number of people flying has brought a sharper focus on passenger issues. Consumers in all sectors feel more empowered in expecting high levels of personal attention and customer service, and more confident in making complaints. Airlines and airports need to respond to this wider trend. And with more elderly and mobility impaired people flying, the industry will come under increasing pressure to raise standards of passenger care.

European Community legislation already regulates the provision of package travel, compensation for denied boarding, carrier liability in the event of accidents or loss or damage to baggage, and Computer Reservation Systems. In the future this coverage is expected to extend to the treatment of passengers subject to cancellation and delays, and the provision of consumer reports on airline performance so that passengers can make informed choices between them.

Within the UK, further action to promote and strengthen consumer interests will include: reviewing the Air Travel Organisers' Licensing arrangements in the light of the CAA's current consultation on financial protection for air travellers and package holidaymakers; seeking statutory powers to impose a new levy to ensure future solvency of the Air Travel Trust Fund; retaining the Air Transport Users Council as the organisation representing the interests of air passengers; working closely with the industry, the police and other interested parties to minimise the amount of disruptive behaviour on board aircraft, including maintaining the Government's unified incident-reporting scheme; working closely with the CAA's new specialist unit on aviation health issues, promoting research, and keeping advice to passengers and crew up to date; and the work of the Office of Fair Trading in promoting consumer choice.

Aviation and Tourism in UK

Consumers have benefited greatly from the growth in foreign travel. Today, UK residents make around 60 million visits overseas each year, compared to just thirteen million in 1978. Around 80 per cent of these are by air.

In-bound tourism accounts for an estimated 4.4 per cent of GDP in 2002, and more than two million direct jobs. Outbound tourism too, although sometimes presented as encouraging people to holiday abroad to the detriment of the domestic economy, also contributes significantly to the economy through revenue earned by tour operators and the air transport sector.

The Government, working with VisitBritain and the Tourism Alliance, has launched a series of recent programmes and campaigns to attract foreign visitors and encourage domestic tourism, in the face of a widening gap in the tourism balance of payments. Britain can compete on its strengths while at the same time enabling British people to holiday abroad and gain from the revenue this generates for British tour operators, airlines, airports and other services. British travellers have little alternative to air travel for long-haul, and many short-haul, destinations, and limits on air capacity would greatly disadvantage incoming tourism, through decisions by travellers from overseas to switch to more convenient and lower-cost destinations away from the UK.

Airports and regional economies

Airports are an important focus for the development of local and regional economies. They attract business and generate employment and open up wider markets. They can provide an important impetus to regeneration and a focus for new commercial and industrial development. And they are increasingly important transport hubs, especially for the logistics industry.

Many airports increasingly act as a focal point for 'clusters' of business development. By offering the potential for the rapid delivery of products by air freight and convenient access to international markets through the availability of flights for business travel, they can attract inward investment to a region.

Some airport clusters, such as those in the West of Scotland or at Bournemouth airport, relate directly to the provision of aviation-related services, such as aircraft maintenance and aeronautical components. At present, however, the majority of indirect employment associated with the supply of goods and services to airports and the airlines which operate from them is located in the South East of England. Building local supply chains and capacity for the aviation industry, including the promotion of Centres of Excellence for aircraft maintenance (see box), could bring important benefits to the economies of regions, as well as assisting the airports and airlines that serve them.

For all these reasons, it is essential that proposals for new airport capacity and related development both reflect, and are reflected in, the spatial development, transport and economic strategies of the English regions and Scotland, Wales and Northern Ireland. The Government expects the relevant English regional bodies to take the conclusions in this White Paper fully into account in drawing up their strategies, and the devolved administrations are encouraged to do the same.

Developing the aircraft maintenance

The UK's leading role in commercial air transport has resulted in the development of an extensive maintenance, repair and overhaul sector in this country. This includes a number of specialist independent, companies who can offer airlines the opportunity to outsource maintenance work, if they need to concentrate on their core business activities and reduce their fixed costs.

As well as serving domestic airlines, maintenance companies based in the UK are well placed to attract business from overseas carriers, based on comparative costs, geography, skills and reputation. The UK currently has some 20 per cent of the European market; and with the world's commercial airliner fleet expected to double over the next twenty years there is a significant opportunity to expand the sector by maintaining or increasing the UK's share of this business.

At the same time, there are concerns about the industry's ability to provide sufficient numbers of licensed engineers and other well-qualified technical personnel to meet the industry's longterm need. This is particularly the case in the South East where the majority of maintenance operations are currently concentrated, but where living costs and wage levels are rising fastest.

The Government therefore wishes to promote the establishment of a number of Centres of Excellence in civil aircraft engineering and training at airports outside the South East of England. This would have a number of advantages: encouraging the growth of this sector, and of the UK's share of an increasing global market; increasing competitiveness as a result of lower labour and facilities costs outside the South East, increasing the supply of well-trained engineers and technicians for the industry as a whole (including operations based in the South East); encouraging the growth and economic benefits of regional airports; and reducing pressures at the busy London airports, so freeing up space for additional passenger and freight facilities.

There are already well-developed proposals for Centres of Excellence in the West of Scotland and the North East, and the concept is being examined in South

Wales. But the opportunity exists to extend the idea to other airports, particularly where they can build upon established maintenance facilities or aerospace clusters.

The Department for Transport will work with other Government departments, devolved administrations, skills agencies, regional bodies and the industry to develop these ideas further and facilitate their implementation.

Air freight

Airports play an increasingly important role in the supply and distribution of goods within their regions. At major airports, such as Heathrow, Gatwick and Manchester, freight is predominantly moved in the holds of passenger aircraft ('bellyhold'), but other airports also cater for dedicated freight-only aircraft. Stansted and East Midlands are the UK's largest freighter airports, and Edinburgh, Glasgow Prestwick and Belfast International also have important roles serving regional markets.

The speed of delivery that air freight can offer is an increasingly important factor for many modern businesses, especially where just-in-time practices and high value commodities are concerned. Work carried out in connection with the consultation exercise suggests that specialist express carriers could account for over 50 per cent of the air freight market by 2030.

The ability to meet the world-wide rapid delivery and logistics requirements of modern businesses is an important factor in assuring the future competitiveness of economies. The Government wishes to ensure that there are airports able to accommodate the anticipated growth in demand in this area, subject to the satisfactory resolution of environmental concerns, especially in respect of night noise.

Growing regional airports

Most airports serve local demand, generally from within their own region. However, larger airports, such as Manchester and Birmingham and a number of those in the South East, also attract passengers from a wider area. These airports provide services to more destinations - some of which would not be viable from smaller airports - and also offer more frequent services.

The major London airports play a dual role. Around 80 per cent of their passenger traffic3 has an origin or destination in London, the South East or the East of England. These regions have a very high level of demand for air travel, accounting for nearly half the total demand. This enables airlines to offer a very wide range of destinations from the London airports, with frequent services, and with two or more competing airlines on most routes. As a result, Heathrow, Gatwick, and increasingly Stansted also, play a national role as a well as a regional one. Many travellers from other parts of the UK fly to one of these London airports in order to catch connecting flights. And many travellers from Wales, the Midlands and parts of the South West travel by road or rail to the major London airports.

The demand for passenger air travel is growing fastest outside the South East, and this trend is expected to continue. As a result, airlines should be able over time to offer direct services to more destinations from a wider range of airports.

The recent emergence of 'no-frills' services, offering a new model of service provision, has stimulated demand across the country, but has been a particularly important factor in the growth that has occurred over the last ten years at many regional airports. Apart from bringing air travel within the reach of more people, it has opened up new routes and destinations. The 'no-frills' sector throughout the UK has expanded from carrying under eight million passengers a year in 1998 to 35 million in 2002, and a projected 47 million in 2003.

The Government's policy is to encourage the growth of regional airports to serve regional and local demand, subject to environmental constraints. This will have a number of benefits, including: supporting the growth of the economies of Scotland, Wales, Northern Ireland and the English regions; relieving congestion at more overcrowded airports, particularly in the South East, and therefore making better use of existing capacity; reducing the need for long-distance travel to and from airports; and giving passengers greater choice.

It is likely that the Government's policy of encouraging the growth of regional airports will have some impact on demand at airports in the South East. The predominant role of South East airports is, however, also a regional one (over 80 per cent of their terminal passenger demand being South East based). The development of regional airports will therefore not have a material impact on demand for additional capacity in the South East.

A key issue for Scotland, Northern Ireland, the North of England and parts of South West England is the availability of landing and take-off 'slots' at other airports, particularly the major London airports. At congested airports in the UK, where demand for slots exceeds supply, slot allocation is governed by EU law and implemented by a slot co-ordinator who is required to act in an independent manner.

Slot allocation regime

EU Regulation 95/93 provides common rules throughout Europe. These are aimed at ensuring neutral, transparent and non-discriminatory allocation, and at providing some certainty for airlines, whilst encouraging competition.

The Regulation allows airlines to retain slots allocated to them by the co-ordinator provided they used them for 80 per cent of the previous equivalent season. When new slots become available, either as a result of new capacity being provided or because existing slots are handed back to the pool by airlines which no longer require them, some priority is given to new entrants.

Slot allocation at Heathrow, Gatwick, Manchester, Birmingham, Glasgow and Stansted is carried out by a company approved for the purpose by the Secretary of State for Transport. The pressure on slots in the UK has led to the development of a 'grey market' in which airlines trade slots with one another in order to increase their holdings or obtain more attractive slots that would not otherwise become available through the pool. This gives airlines commercial flexibility, enabling them to acquire additional or more attractive slots. UK and foreign airlines have been able to secure slots at Heathrow and Gatwick airports by trading and acquiring interests so as to provide services better suited to the needs of consumers.

The current allocation system contains fundamental weaknesses. The majority of slots at congested airports are awarded on the basis of historic use - so-called 'grandfather rights', and not in ways that reflect their true value or benefits to consumers and the economy. The Government wishes to see a slot allocation system that encourages the more efficient use of scarce capacity. At congested airports a transparent, market-based approach should offer the best solution; and that if airlines' decisions on slots reflect consumers' preferences, as expressed in their willingness to pay for flights, this should maximise benefits to consumers.

Iin deciding whether to buy or sell slots, airlines will not take into account all the wider economic and other benefits that domestic air services to London may bring to other parts of the UK. The Government notes that the

Route Development Fund established by the Scottish Executive in November 2002 has been very successful, having already helped to deliver fifteen new routes from Scottish Airports, bringing the prospect of substantial benefits to Scotland's economy.

The establishment of further funds in Wales and in English regions outside the South East and East of England could play a valuable role in establishing new direct business links from both primary and secondary airports in these areas, thus stimulating inward investment and tourism.

Any such fund will need to comply with UK and European Union law, especially in respect of state aids and competition. In particular, ensuring transparency and non-discrimination will be essential. The Department for Transport will accordingly continue to monitor and offer guidance on the structure and operation of the existing funds and any others that are brought forward in order to: ensure compatibility with EC guidelines; address any problems that may emerge; and keep under review the contribution they are making to regional economic development targets.

In addition, and recognising the importance of regional services, the Government is prepared to intervene in well defined circumstances to protect slots at the London airports for such services by imposing Public Service Obligations (PSOs). The imposition of a PSO enables the slots used for that service to be 'ring-fenced', so that an airline cannot use them for a service to an alternative destination. The rules for imposing PSOs are set out in European regulations.

The Government will work closely with the European Commission and other Member States with the aim of ensuring that any amendments to the regulations will recognise the importance of regional access to London airports. In the interim, it will be necessary to develop clear guidelines so that any applications for the imposition of PSOs on routes from regional airports into London can be processed in an objective and transparent manner. For the purposes of this policy, London airports will include Gatwick, Heathrow, London City, Luton and Stansted.

Under current Community law it is not possible to impose a PSO on a route between two cities or regions on which adequate services are already being operated commercially and the airline concerned has no intention of withdrawing from the route.Where there is an existing service, PSOs would be imposed only when an airline's withdrawal from a currently operated route would reduce the frequency level below an adequate level. Airlines currently operating services to London airports will be asked to provide the Government with at least four months' notice of their intention to withdraw from a route or reduce frequencies if, as a consequence of such withdrawal or reduction in service, the overall level of service went below an adequate level.

Demonstrating the importance of the service to the economic development of the region concerned will be the responsibility of local bodies such as the relevant Devolved Administration, Regional Development Agency or local authority. It will also be for these bodies to reimburse the Department for Transport for any funds provided for subsidies, should these be required.

Long-distance rail alternatives

Passengers on internal flights currently account for some thirteen per cent of total traffic at UK airports. Most of them are on flights between the London airports and other parts of the UK. These services are important for point-to-point traffic, especially to and from Scotland, Northern Ireland, the North of England and parts of the South West, but also for passengers wishing to connect with onward flights or reach destinations in the South East outside central London.

Studies suggest that rail competes well with air on point-to-point journeys of two to three hours. So rail is, for example, the preferred option for inter-urban travel between London and the Midlands. But for longer journeys air travel is the mode of choice. For example, comparing business trips by rail or by air from Scotland to London and the South East, the overwhelming majority - some 93 per cent - are by air.

Investments to improve the inter-urban rail network will, over time, increase the attractiveness of rail as an alternative, as will more attractive pricing packages from rail operators. Work already in hand on up-grading the West Coast Main Line will, for example, cut journey times between Manchester and Central London by half an hour, and between Glasgow and London by 45 minutes, and enable more frequent and reliable services. The completion of the new High-Speed Channel Tunnel Rail Link in 2007 will further enhance the competitiveness of rail for some journeys between London and Northern European cities (see box). Looking further ahead, there are plans for improvements to the East Coast Main Line, and the Strategic Rail Authority is considering the feasibility of proposals for a new high-speed North-South rail line.

Eurostar

Eurostar has provided an attractive alternative to short-haul air services to the continent. It has already secured some 60 per cent of the market on the London-Paris route, and 50 per cent on the London-Brussels route. There are at least a million fewer air passengers a year on these routes since the introduction of Eurostar and Shuttle rail services. The first phase of the Channel Tunnel Rail Link opened in September 2003. Completion in 2007 will see the fastest journey time between London and Paris cut to two and a quarter hours and between London and Brussels to two hours, making rail an even more attractive choice for these routes.

In bringing forward proposals for new airport capacity, operators will need to have regard, where appropriate, to the potential impact of new rail investment on demand for air travel. The introduction of high-speed rail lines in France has had a dramatic effect on domestic air services on individual short routes, although it has had a relatively modest effect on air traffic overall. For the UK, on specific routes, and particularly for city-centre to city-centre journeys, it might cause some reduction in service frequency or aircraft size. But for other long-distance journeys, including interlining (travel to connecting flights), rail is unlikely to be the most attractive choice. And for some parts of the UK, travel by air will remain the only realistic option.

New investment in rail capacity will see more long-distance journeys by rail. But the majority of this increase is expected to come through switching from car travel or as a result of new demand. Work undertaken by the Strategic Rail Authority suggests that the number of passengers switching from air to rail as a result of planned improvements to the West and East Coast Main Lines will be around 25 per cent from Manchester, ten to fifteen per cent from the North East, and less than five per cent from Scotland. These switches will be welcome, particularly during the next few years when runway capacity at the major London airports will be in short supply; but they are not expected to affect future passenger demand at the most crowded airports by more than a few percentage points.

Access to and from airports

Ensuring easy and reliable access for passengers, which minimises environmental, congestion and other local impacts, is a key factor in considering any proposal for new airport capacity. All such proposals must be accompanied by clear proposals on surface access which meet these criteria.

Increasing the proportion of passengers who get to airports by public transport can help reduce road congestion and air pollution. Airports are part of the national transport infrastructure, and need to be planned and developed in that context. The Strategic Rail Authority and (for strategic roads within England) the Highways Agency will take full account of likely future airport development, and regional and local transport strategies should do the same.

The Government expects developers to pay the costs of up-grading or enhancing road, rail or other transport networks or services where these are needed to cope with additional passengers travelling to and from expanded or growing airports. Where the scheme has a wider range of beneficiaries, the Government, along with the devolved administrations, the Strategic Rail Authority, the Highways Agency and local authorities, will consider the need for additional public funding through their investment programmes on a case-by-case basis. Prospective developers should consult those bodies at an early stage in formulating their proposals.

3

AIR TRAVEL FARES AND
TICKETING RULES

Airlines assign prices to their services in an attempt to maximize profitability. To do this well requires yield management technology and pricing flexibility. They use differentiated pricing, a form of price discrimination, in order to sell air services at varying prices simultaneously to different segments. Factors influencing the price include the days remaining until departure, the current booked load factor, the forecast of total demand by price point, competitive pricing in force, and variations by day of week of departure and by time of day.

A complicating factor is that of origin-destination control ("O&D control"). Someone purchasing a ticket from say, Melbourne to Sydney for $A200 is competing with someone else who wants to fly Melbourne to Los Angeles through Sydney on the same airplane, and who is willing to pay $A1400. Should the airline prefer the $A1400 passenger, or the $A200 passenger + a possible Sydney-Los Angeles passenger willing to pay $A1300? Airlines have to make hundreds of thousands of similar pricing decisions daily in their markets. In contrast, low fare carriers usually offer straightforward, preannounced, simple prices. They can do this by quoting prices for each leg of a trip; passengers simply add them together to construct a full journey.

The advent of advanced computerized reservations systems in the late 1970s, most notably Sabre, allowed airlines to easily perform cost-benefit analyses on different pricing structures, leading to almost perfect price discrimination in some cases (that is, filling each seat on an aircraft at the highest price that can be charged without driving the consumer elsewhere). The intense nature of airfare pricing has led to the term "fare war" to describe efforts by airlines to undercut other airlines on competitive routes.

Computers also allow airlines to predict, with some accuracy, how many passengers will actually fly after making a reservation to fly. This allows airlines to overbook their flights enough to fill the aircraft while accounting for "no-shows," but not enough (in most cases) to force paying passengers off the aircraft for lack of seats. Since an average of 1/3 of all seats are flown empty, stimulative pricing for low demand flights coupled with overbooking on high demand flights can help reduce this figure.

AIR FARES

Trying to understand all the different fares offered by the nation's airlines is a daunting task. That's because the major carriers have created fare schedules every bit as complex as the federal tax code. So many different fares are available it's unlikely that any two passengers on a given flight will pay the same price for their tickets.

Airlines determine fare pricing based on a number of factors, such as the number of seats in each fare category, reservation time periods, competitor pricing on similar flights, and the type of consumers using a particular flight. Computer-assisted revenue management systems are used to examine historical demand to establish the number of seats made available for sale at various fares. Analysts then monitor each flight to adjust seat allocations and fares accordingly.

That said, there are really only four types of fares-although these fares are constantly being adjusted by the airlines' revenue management systems. These fare types include

— *Unrestricted*: These fares have no or limited restrictions on getting refunds on cancelled flights or making changes to your original itinerary. Because they allow the greatest flexibility (and sometimes offer other perks), these are the highest priced fares on any given flight and the benchmark from which other fares are discounted. They are often referred to as "walk-up" fares.

— *Restricted*: These fares have advance purchase requirements, restrictions on the use of the ticket, and penalties for changes to the original ticket. Because they limit your travel and reservation options and impose penalties for change, these tickets are sold at a discount to unrestricted fares on the same flight. Discount fares typically have advance purchase requirements of 3, 7, 14, or 21 days; Saturday night stay requirements; and minimum or maximum stay restrictions.

— *Capacity controlled*: These fares, offered by discount carriers are created when an airline sets aside a limited number of seats at a specific price. So, although you may not have to purchase the ticket a set number of days in advance, the fare might not be available if you wait too long to make your purchase. This is also a common practice used to book flights using frequent flyer miles.

— *Internet-only*: These are discounted restricted fares only available for purchase from the airline's Web site. To encourage you to book directly with them online, airlines may promise that their lowest fares are available only on the their Web sites.

Just because you purchase a ticket well in advance does not guarantee you the lowest price; airlines often lower their fares midstream.

A new trend in the industry is to announce new lower unrestricted fares-a way of reducing prices for business travelers without changing the underlying fare schedule. Airlines are also introducing lower one-way "walk-up" fares, for tickets purchased on the day of the flight. Overall, the general consensus is that given the growth of low-fare carriers, fares for business travelers are getting lower.

CLASSES OF SERVICE

There are four fare classes of service-first, business, economy plus, and economy/coach. Most of the major carriers offer at least two classes of service on their flights. Low-fare and regional carriers may only sell coach class. Some low-fare carriers, such as AirTran, only sell one-way tickets, which is important to keep in mind if you are booking your flight online.

RIGHTS, RULES, AND PROMISES

When you purchase an airline ticket you are agreeing to the airline's Conditions of Carriage. This is a legally binding document that details the services the airline is required to offer and the rules to which you are required to adhere. This detailed and complicated document covers everything from ticket validity, baggage, wait lists, flight delays and cancellations, refunds, and rerouting. You will find it on the inside cover of your ticket jacket.

The Aviation Consumer Protection Division is the government organization responsible for receiving consumer complaints. This organization does a good job of simplifying air travel rights in its publication, Flight-Rights, A Consumers Guide to Air Travel. This document is available on their web site. In September 1999, the 14 largest U.S. airlines-all members of the Air Transport Association-released customer service plans that describe new customer service "commitments." The prototype plan has 11 points describing the practices airlines promise, but are not legally obligated, to follow.

Each airline has its own version of this document. The following summarizes some key points common to these plans:

— Allow customers 24 hours from initial reservation to change travel plans without penalty.

— Offer the lowest fare for which the customer is eligible.

— Provide food, water, restrooms, and medical treatment for passengers on board a grounded aircraft.

— Disclose to passengers on request whether a flight is overbooked.

— Give accurate and timely information on flight delays and cancellations.

— Provide on-time baggage delivery.

— Provide information and policies about oversold flights.

Ticket Validity

In general, your ticket is valid for travel only when used in accordance with all terms and conditions of sale outlined in the Conditions of Carriage. Your ticket is invalid if any of the following conditions apply:

— The ticket is used for travel to a destination other than that specified on the ticket.

— You fail to comply with applicable stay-over requirements.

— You do not meet the purpose or status requirement associated with the fare category on the ticket.

— The airline determines that the ticket has been purchased or used in a manner designed to circumvent applicable fare rules.

Many travelers, however, have figured out how to purchase restricted tickets but avoid the restrictions. So airlines specifically prohibit the following practices:

— Back-to-back ticketing-The combination of two or more round-trip restricted fares end-to-end for the purpose of circumventing minimum stay requirements.

— Throwaway ticketing-The use of a round-trip excursion fare for one-way travel.

— Hidden city/point beyond ticketing-The purchase of a fare from a point before the passenger's actual origin or to a point beyond the passenger's actual destination.

If you break the rules, the airline has the right to do any or all of the following:

— Cancel any remaining portion of the itinerary.

— Confiscate unused flight coupons.

— Refuse to let you board or check your luggage.

— Charge you for the remaining value of the ticket, which is no less than the difference between the fare actually paid and the lowest fare applicable to your actual itinerary.

OVERBOOKING

Airlines routinely overbook their flights-that is, they sell more seats than are actually available. They do this because people typically do not cancel their reservations when they change their travel plans; if the airlines didn't overbook, they'd have a lot of empty seats on all their flights. Fortunately, it all works out-most of the time. The airline overbooks a percentage of the available seats, and a similar percentage of passengers are no-shows. More often than not, everybody who shows up gets a seat.

In those rare instances where the flight actually has more real passengers than seats, the airline will ask for volunteers who are willing to give up their seats in exchange for compensation-typically a coupon for free travel and a seat on a later flight. This practice is known as voluntary denied boarding. If there are not enough volunteers, airlines will deny boarding to selected passengers. This practice is known as involuntary denied boarding and is likely to make you irate if you're one of the involunteers. Overall, less than 1% of passengers are denied boarding, either voluntarily or involuntarily.

If you are considering giving up your seat on an overbooked flight, keep these points in mind:

— If there aren't enough volunteers, you can try to negotiate for a better deal.

— Before you give up your original seat, ask for a confirmed seat on the next flight.

— Ask about any restrictions on your free ticket.

— Ask what the airline will do for you while you wait for the next flight-you can sometimes get the carrier to pay for a meal or hotel room.

Each airline has its own policy. For example, American Airlines states: "We will usually deny boarding based upon check-in time, but we may also consider factors such as severe hardships, fare paid, and status within the AAdvantage program." Southwest Airlines states: "Carrier shall deny boarding in reverse order from the order in which passengers checked in at the gate, with no preference given to any particular person or category of passenger."

If you get bumped you are entitled to an on-the-spot payment of denied boarding compensation. The amount depends on the price of your ticket and the length of the delay, as follows:

— If the airline arranges substitute transportation that is scheduled to arrive at your destination 1 to 2 hours after your original arrival time (1 to 4 hours on international flights), the airline must pay you an amount equal to your one-way fare to your final destination.

— If the substitute transportation is scheduled to get you to your destination more than 2 hours later (4 hours internationally), or if the airline does not make any substitute travel arrangements for you, the compensation doubles to 200% of your fare.

— You always get to keep your original ticket and use it on another flight. If you choose to make your own arrangements, you can request an "involuntary refund" for the ticket for the flight you were bumped from. The denied boarding compensation is essentially a payment for your inconvenience.

Conditions and exceptions to the preceding are as follows:

— To be eligible for compensation, you must have a confirmed reservation.

— You must meet the airline's deadline for buying your ticket and check-in deadline.

— No compensation is due if the airline arranges substitute transportation that is scheduled to arrive at your destination within 1 hour of your originally scheduled arrival time.

— If the airline must substitute a smaller plane for the one it originally planned to use, the carrier isn't required to pay people who are bumped as a result.

— The rules do not apply to charter flights, or to scheduled flights operated with planes that hold 60 or fewer passengers.

DELAYS AND CANCELLATIONS

It is important to remember that airlines don't guarantee their schedules. Unlike the practice of involuntary denied boarding, there is no federal requirement for policies regarding delayed and cancelled flights. Instead, each airline has its own policy. For major carriers, the typical policy states that if your flight cancellation/delay was not due to weather, terrorism, labor disputes, or other "force majeure" events (in other words, something the airline could not control), the airline must confirm you on the next flight to your destination at no additional cost-or refund your ticket, even if it is nonrefundable. In practice, most airlines will book you on another carrier's flight and provide overnight accomodations if you can't get to your final destination on the expected arrival day. If you are delayed, ask the airline staff if they will pay for meals or a phone call.

Changing Your Ticket

If you purchased an unrestricted, refundable fare and need to change your flight, you are good to go. However, if you've opted to buy a restricted ticket and want to change your reservation, fly standby on an earlier flight, or upgrade to a higher fare class, remember that fees for reservation changes, same-day standby, and upgrades will probably apply-and that these fees and policies vary by airline.

Cancellation/Change Fees

Airlines charge a fee-called a change fee-if you want to change your restricted-fare itinerary. These change fees are in addition to any difference between the cost of the original ticket and the cost of the new fare.

Same-Day Standby

Policies for flying same-day standby (taking an earlier or later flight on the same day as your original reservation) vary by airline and fare. If you think you might want to fly on a different flight on the same day, call the airline and tell them you are thinking of flying standby. They can examine the flight's load factor and give you a fairly good idea of your chances of getting a seat.

Because most airlines allow you to fly standby at no additional cost, the advantage of flying standby instead of changing your reservation is that if you have purchased a restricted fare you can avoid the change fee-and any applicable fare increase. However, there are exceptions. If you are holding a flight-specific fare ticket, you may be prohibited from flying standby, even if there is space available.

Upgrading

Upgrades are coupons that allow you to move from a lower class of service (such as coach) to a higher class of service (business or first class), if there are available seats. Many people upgrade because using a coupon is cheaper than purchasing a confirmed business or first class ticket; the caveat is that you are not guaranteed seat availability.

There are typically three ways to upgrade your class of service: purchase an upgrade, qualify for a free upgrade, or use frequent flyer miles to upgrade. The fees and rules for upgrading vary by airline and can be complicated.

Most airlines do not allow upgrades on discounted fares. They tend to allocate upgrades based on your fare and status in their frequent flyer program; elite members are placed first in line for available seats. In addition, most airlines limit the time periods in which you can either pay cash or use your miles to upgrade. For example, American Airlines allows Executive Platinum members to request upgrades 100 hours before a flight, whereas Gold-level members have to wait until 24 hours before the flight.

When it comes to receiving free upgrades, these are most often reserved for elite-level frequent flyers. One notable exception is Northwest's ConnectFirst fare, which gives free upgrades to passengers flying full-fare coach tickets, if seats are available.

If you want to use your frequent flyer miles to purchase an upgrade, your fare will likely determine how many miles you need. For example, US Airways requires 10,000 miles to upgrade from a full-fare ticket-but 20,000 to upgrade from a restricted fare. Continental Airlines only allows elite-level members and those using frequent flyer miles to upgrade.

4

AIR TRAVEL CONSOLIDATORS

In essence air travel consolidators enable travellers to compare flight prices across a range of airlines for a particular flight route on at the same time period. This enables travellers to save time and money by comparing a range of airlines simultaneously to determine not only the most cost effective airline, but also the most convenient time to travel and airline to travel from/to where there are several options.

The core benefit of using an air travel consolidator is that you can inevitably find not only the cheapest flight route, but also the most affordable flight at the most convenient time.

As the online travel market has grown over the last decade, so the number of travel consolidators on the net likewise has increased, and is due to eclipse traditional offline travel consolidators within the next two years.

Indeed, the benefit of using an online air travel consolidator is that you are able to not only compare several airlines using one consolidator, but in fact quickly and conveniently compare several travel consolidators' best prices for a particular travel route against one another. As such you are effectively comparing 'the best quote' across a range of 'best airfare' quote providers.

While many online air travel consolidators may offer the same flight routes by the same airline, the relationship and deals that they have which airline will inevitably vary, as such one consolidator will be able to quote a far more cost effective price on the same flight as another airline.

TRADITIONAL AIR TRAVEL CONSOLIDATORS

There are three main types of airfare consolidators:

Destination Specialists

Specialising in a particular region, these consolidators are able to negotiate strong discounts for flights to particular destinations. Usually, these type of consolidators often cross sell their flights as packages with hotel and/or car hire to maximise their commissions, and often use the flight as a loss leader. Naturally, as they tend to send a high volume of travellers on particular routes with their chosen airline partners they are able to get great deals on flights to particular destinations.

Wholesale consolidators

While you won't normally have any contact with these type of consolidators they inevitably will be the company your high-street travel agent contacts to find the best deal on a particular flight route.

These consolidators operate huge volumes of sales on extremely low margins to a wide range of travel agents. By bringing together a range of travel agents they are able to provide best airfares for thousands of travellers and thus negotiate stronger airfare rates than a single travel agent could negotiate.

It is rare that such consolidators ever sell air tickets directly to the public as their margins are unable to accommodate customer service on a large scale.

Multi-Stop/Round the World Specialists

Most air consolidators struggle to give really competitive rates on multi-stop and 'round the world' flights as they tend to calculate costs by combining single trip airfares which can be the most expensive way to book several flights.

Multi-stop specialists are capable of accommodating a combination of single flights by negotiating special deals with larger airlines which serve multiple destinations.

ONLINE TRAVEL CONSOLIDATORS

The internet is arguably the best place to find the cheapest airfares nowadays. While they lack the attention and service of a traditional travel agent, the ease of price comparison cannot be beaten. Online travel consolidators tend to be able to undercut traditional agents simply because, they can afford to market to a wider audience online to attract more customers and can cut their overheads by avoiding the expensive high-street rents that travel agents must absorb.

— *Expedia* - Arguably the net's biggest travel consolidator offering special flight prices with hundreds of airlines across the globe.

— *Travelocity* - searches the lowest fares from hundreds of airlines, and gives you access to Web Fares from all six major airlines. Choose your plane seat with Seat Maps, and know when fares to your favorite destinations drop with Fare Watcher.

— *Travel Supermarket* - Flight comparison engine from the same people responsible for Money Supermarket, finance comparison engine. What separates this engine from other European-focussed airfare consolidators is that it provides flight comparison for budget airlines which tend not to be featured on some of the bigger flight consolidators. Also enables you to submit multiple departure airports for the same flight. Orbitz - Award-winning flight search engine makes it easy to find the lowest fares on more than 455 airlines.

— *Skyscanner* - Ues search engine technology to obtain ticket information from airline websites. This provides visitors with a single place where they can find flight prices for budget airlines throughout Europe, and enables travelers to quickly compare airfare prices on a route across a range of departure dates.

— *Cheap Flights* - With more than 700 travel companies displaying over one million deals each day, Cheapflights is also the UK's most complete travel portal displaying great bargains on flights to destinations throughout the world.

— *STA Travel* - Student specialist offering discount flight deals for students and travellers under 26. STA Travel compares flight prices across all major airline groups.

In addition to finding a good online air fare ticket consolidator, it is possible to get a cheaper airfare by taking into consideration the yield management system that is used to calculate your airfare. While, it is near impossible to work out the system that each airline works on, it is of interest to have a broader understanding of the pricing structure used to determine your flight ticket price as this is a base upon which your consolidator will take its own commission.

A yield management system is designed to calculate the optimum selling price of an airfare based upon a range of variable factors which will influence the popularity of any given flight route at any time in the year, thus influencing factors include the time of the flight, season, local events at the point of departure and arrival and the pricing patterns of competing airlines.

The demand for any particular flight is based upon such factors which are then applied to a base flight rate, thus certain flights may cost 120% the base rate, whereas other may cost 50% of the base rate depending the time of year etc.

Utilising figures from similar flights, airlines are then able to predict the demand for a particular flight which will determine the rate at which they expect to sell tickets for the flight. If tickets are selling slowly, then they may modify the prices to realign there selling expectations for the flight as it nears the date of departure. Naturally all these metrics are perpetually changing, so calculating the optimum time to buy a ticket is notoriously difficult.

Nevertheless, while it is potentially possible to get great deals at the very last minute, the safest option is to buy your ticket as early as possible. One thing that is for certain is that you are unlikely to have paid the same price for your ticket as the person sitting next to you.

MEDIA'S CONTRIBUTION TO TRAVEL DITSRIBUTION

It's taken years for travel suppliers to understand the customer. Remember the first generation of airline and hotel Websites? Online booking interfaces were designed from the "inside out": designed as if an airline employee or travel agent would be using them, with airport codes and expressions like "rack rates" all part the standard customer interface. But suppliers quickly learned the value of user centered design, usability testing, and designing intuitive and simple interfaces. The second and current generation of travel tools and Websites are straightforward and clear, and as a result, they have been enormously successful.

As the tools became easier to use -and as millions of customers began using the Web-the travel industry experienced a huge evolution. Online travel booking was no longer just for the early adopter, but for any consumer who was comfortable purchasing products over the Web. For those customers (and the new users to the Internet who are following right behind them) the industry has forever changed distribution through changing customer behavior. This change in customer behavior is a huge achievement for the travel industry.

Today, the reliance on travel agents for booking simple products and itineraries has evaporated, and the use of travel agents is generally reserved for complicated itineraries, destination consulting, and corporate travel (where online tools have not yet been deployed). Future changes in online distribution can now occur at a more rapid pace, given that customers are already comfortable using, comparing, and experimenting with online travel services. And for those users who are still behind the curve and have not yet purchased travel online, it is just a matter of time.

In addition to this fundamental change in customer behavior, another change in the industry has helped prime us for the next revolution: the rapid adoption of high speed internet connections. Within the last few years, more than 22 million American homes have now connected to the Internet via high-speed connections (DSL or cable modems), and more will follow. Whether at home or at the office, using the Web is now largely an instantaneous, high-speed experience.

Travel planning is inherently 'experiential'. As part of their planning process, customers continually search for as much detail on what type of experience they will be having on their trip before and after they make their booking. Using rich media/rich content is a very effective way of conveying very detailed travel information. If a picture is worth a thousand words, then rich media -in selling travel solutions-speaks volumes.

Whether a customer is booking a holiday and wants detailed views of the resort's pool, or she is traveling for business and wants to see the details of the fitness center that she will be using for the next two weeks, rich media will help answer those questions, allay fears, and close the sale.

Similar to CRM, most of the early experiments into rich media online focused too much on the technology itself, and not on how the technology will add real value to the business. In the case of rich media, suppliers need to consider how rich media will enhance the customer experience, while considering the cost of creating and updating the content. Spinning logos might be fun for a developer to create, but they don't add real value to a customer experience.

To date, the travel industry has been slow to incorporate rich media into their online services. Other industries, like the automotive industry, have been much more forward-thinking. As automotive manufacturers have realized the importance their Web sites have in consumer's pre-purchase research process, they have been the first major industry to exploit the power of rich media. Cars are similar to travel products in the sense that both are "complex" products, where customer research and comparison can occur over a longer pre-purchase research period. And like travel, cars have complex sets of features that typically need to be explained or illustrated to customers.

Rich media is about to change the online travel marketplace. The first and second generation travel tools have focused on making online services usable. With the new possibilities of rich media over high speed connections, a new chapter will be written on how rich media helped online travel solutions enter a new era of usefulness, conveying a whole new dimension of information.

Unlike the flat Websites of today, rich media will have the ability to:

— *Inspire* : As rich media is deployed and online sites become more immersive, online travel tools will have the power to inspire users, something that has been very difficult with even the best of today's flat Web sites. Some examples of how rich media can inspire customers: a well designed inspirational online experience might just help the customer choose one holiday resort over another. In addition, an engaging online feature that brings to life the excitement of South Beach can encourage some customers to plan a trip for an upcoming weekend for which they have no plans and weren't considering traveling.

— *Illustrate* : Rich media can convey information that is sometimes very hard to articulate or describe, Images, Video, Virtual Tours, and Audio all have the power to help convey far more accurate, detailed, and emotional travel information. Consider the following opportunities:

  — *Airlines* - For the valued long-haul business class passenger, a virtual tour of the airport lounge and the flatbed business cabin could help translate the elegance of the real-world experience into the online experience.

  — *Hotels* - Holiday planners can better help evaluate -at a detailed level- the different amenities of resorts "

  — *Cruises* - A successful cruise hinges on enjoying the on-board experience.

— *Simplify* : When properly designed, rich media interfaces can help simplify the interaction with applications that are typically difficult to use. Free from some of the limits of HTML, rich media can bridge the connections to multiple back-end systems to allow side-by-side comparisons or show real-time availability of inventory.

To date, the travel industry has been slow to deploy rich media, and for some great reasons. Early attempts at using rich media were largely gratuitous, ineffective, and costly. Things are starting to change. The Broadmoor Hotel is one of the first suppliers to use a Flash based interface to their reservation engine. Although the redesign successfully shortened the number of screens typically needed to complete a hotel booking, the interface is very complicated.

And while Broadmoor's interface is a interesting experiment, sadly it highlights some of the pitfalls in designing for rich media. Broadmoor has deployed a rich media interface that seems aimed at designers and Internet professionals. Any user with only moderate skills or confidence levels in Internet booking would surely be overwhelmed by the complexities of this interface (not to mention the legibility of the type, icons, and interaction design cues). So what benefit has this new interface added to the business? Furthermore, given the critical nature of the booking process, a separate HTML-based booking interface must be maintained.

The Broadmoor interface example raises a number of issues to consider when designing for rich media. First, and foremost, there must be a continued emphasis on good design and usability. Just like the arrival of the laser printer gave everyone the potential to become a desktop publisher, doesn't mean that everyone had skills in page layout. The problems with the next wave of rich media tools will be exponentially more dangerous, since we are dealing with complex interactions. In short, think of the Broadmoor Hotel example and don't create a flight simulator when all you need is a simple interface. The appropriateness of rich media must always be considered.

It's time to think about how rich media will change distribution for your business. Just like how the first and second generation travel Web sites separated the leaders from the laggards in distribution strategies, rich media will begin to identify the next generation of winners in creating a step change in the usefulness and engagement level of online customer experiences. Consider how rich media can change your current online customer experiences and overall distribution strategies.

5

GLOBAL DISTRIBUTION SYSTEMS

A computer reservations system, or CRS, is a computerized system used to store and retrieve information and conduct transactions related to travel. Originally designed and operated by airlines, they were later extended to travel agents as a sales channel; major CRS operations are also known as Global Distribution Systems (GDS). Airlines have divested most of their direct holdings to dedicated Global Distribution System companies, and many systems are now accessible to consumers through Internet gateways for hotel, rental cars, and other services as well as airline tickets.

The big GDS companies are all facing challenges. Their system architectures are largely based on a mainframe TPF (Transaction Processing Facility) framework which — while very reliable, and capable of tremendous I/O throughput – has relatively little CPU power, and is exorbitantly expensive to maintain and enhance. The declining cost of modern server hardware and the relatively recent introduction of pricing, shopping, and booking software from vendors like ITA Software, has allowed many airlines to shift significant buying volume to their own websites, thereby avoiding GDS distribution fees of $4 or more per flight sector.

In recent years, all of the big four GDS companies have, to varying degrees, begun selectively migrating (or "offloading") processes from their legacy mainframe platforms to service oriented architectures (SOA). By utilizing high-performance, lower cost open systems platforms in an SOA approach, they further improve their capacity to cost effectively handle a fast-rising "look-to-book" ratio, i.e., the number of shopping transactions compared to actual purchases. The explosive growth of this ratio was driven initially by the creation and utilization of robotic software and, more recently, by the rapid growth of consumers' multi-site shopping behavior on the Internet.

Beginning in 2004, several companies – including ITA Software, G2 Switchworks, Farelogix, and Innovative Network Systems – claimed to be developing complete GDS alternatives. The new entrants tout lower fees and greater flexibility. Unsurprisingly, the big four GDS companies cast doubt on their viability.

However, it is still very uncommon for a travel agency to operate without the use of at least one of the big four GDS systems. The GDS companies are playing catch up in the technology arena. All now have a browser based system; Sabre, Galileo and Worldspan have full browser based solutions while Amadeus still utilizes a VPN based system. Most, in one way or another, are aggregating webfares back into the GDS, and some airlines have agreed to post their webfares both to their own sites and on the GDS.

Many of these GDS's have now started to integrate forward into the business, reaching out to the customers with their own websites, such as Expedia (owned by IAC, which also owns Amadeus), Travelocity (owned by Sabre), Orbitz (owned by Cendant) and many others. These new entrants to the market have further eroded revenues at the GDS.

Today, each system allows an operator to locate and reserve inventory (for instance, an airline seat on a particular route at a particular time), find and process fares/prices applicable to the inventory (Revenue management, Variable pricing and Geo (marketing)), generate tickets and travel documents, and generate reports on the transactions for accounting or marketing purposes.

HISTORY OF GLOBAL DISTRIBUTION SYSTEMS

In the early days of commercial aviation, passengers were relatively few and each airline's routes and fares were tightly regulated, in the United States by the Civil Aeronautics Board after 1940. These were published in a volume entitled the Official Airline Guide, from which travel agents or consumers could construct an itinerary, then call or telex airline agents who would mark the reservation on a card and file it. As the demand for and complexity of air travel expanded, however, this process soon became onerous and costly.

In 1946, American Airlines installed the first experimental automated booking system, the electromechanical Reservisor. A newer machine with temporary storage based on a magnetic drum soon followed, the Magnetronic Reservisor. This system proved fairly successful, and was soon being used by a number of airlines, Sheraton Hotels, and Goodyear for inventory control. However these systems were seriously hampered by the need for local human operators to do the actual lookups; ticketing agents would have to call into the booking office, whose operators would make requests to a small team operating the Reservisor and then speak the results back into the telephone. There was no way for the agents to directly query the system.

In 1953, Trans-Canada Airlines (TCA) started investigating a computerized system with remote terminals, testing one such concept on the University of Toronto's Manchester Mark I machine that summer. Although successful, they found that input/output was a major problem. Ferranti Canada became involved in the project and suggested a new system using punch cards and a transistorized computer in place of the unreliable tube-based Mark I. The resulting system, ReserVec, started operation in 1962, and took over all booking operations in January 1963. Terminals were placed in all of TCA's ticketing offices, where queries and bookings took about one second to complete with no remote operators needed.

In 1953, American Airlines CEO C. R. Smith chanced to sit next to R. Blair Smith, a senior IBM sales representative. Their idea of an automated airline reservation system (ARS) resulted in a 1959 venture known as the Semi-Automatic Business Research Environment, or SABRE, launched the following year. By the time the network was completed in December 1964 it was the largest non-governmental data processing system in the world.

Other airlines soon established their own systems. Delta Air Lines launched its DATAS in 1968. United Airlines and TWA followed in 1971 with Apollo and PARS respectively. Soon, travel agents began pushing for a system that could automate their side of the process by accessing the various ARSs directly to make reservations. Fearful this would place too much power in the hands of agents, American Airlines executive Robert Crandall proposed creating an industry-wide Computer Reservations System to be a central clearinghouse for U.S. travel; other airlines demurred, citing fear of antitrust prosecution.

In 1976, United began offering its Apollo system to travel agents; while it would allow the agents to book tickets on United's competitors, the marketing value of the convenient terminal proved indispensable. SABRE, PARS, and DATAS were soon released to travel agents as well. Following airline deregulation in 1978, an efficient CRS proved particularly important; by some counts, Texas Air executive Frank Lorenzo purchased money-losing Eastern Air Lines specifically to gain control of its SystemOne CRS.

European airlines also began to invest in the field in the 1980s, propelled by growth in demand for travel as well as technological advances which allowed the GDS to offer ever-increasing services and searching power. In 1987, a consortium led by Air France and West Germany's Lufthansa developed Amadeus, modeled on Eastern's SystemOne. In 1990, Delta, Northwest Airlines, and Trans World Airlines formed Worldspan, and in 1993, another consortium including British Airways, KLM, and United Airlines among others formed competing company, Galileo International, based on United's Apollo network. Numerous smaller companies have also been formed, aimed at geographic, industry, or language niches inadequately served by the "big four."

COMPETITIVE CONCERNS

In Global Distribution Systems, such as Amadeus, Galileo CRS, Worldspan, or Sabre, codeshare results in the same flight details, except for the flight number, being displayed on computer screens excessively forcing other airlines flights to be displayed on following pages where they may be missed by passengers searching for required flights.

Much competition in the airline industry revolves around ticket sales (also known as "seat booking") strategies. Travel agents have a preference for flights which provide a direct connection. Code sharing gives this impression. Computer reservations systems (CRS) also often do not discriminate between direct flights and code sharing flights and present both before options that involve several isolate stretches run by different companies.

Criticism has been levelled against code sharing by consumer organizations and national departments of trade since it is claimed it is confusing and not transparent to passengers, but thus far without any success.

The online travel market continues to evolve, creating both risks and opportunities for shoppers. While a wide variety of ticket-booking sites remain, the market itself has become more concentrated. We see improvements in five key areas: The ability to get low fares, viable itineraries, ease of use, customer service and privacy and security policies. Yet we also see many problems remain to be solved. Some are merely growing pains of a relatively new business. Others reveal challenges created by the underlying characteristics of the travel industry itself.

The traditional travel business, operating between the launch of deregulation in 1978 - the airline deregulation era of the late 1970s - and the onset of online travel in the mid-to-late 1990s, evolved with an integrated group of players - airlines, Computer Reservations Systems, travel agents and credit card companies - whose successes were interdependent. In other words, if an airline sold a seat and made money, so did everyone else in the chain.

But the advent of online travel created new business models that altered the relationships among the key players. They became less interdependent and more competitive. Moreover, their two primary goals were now similar: First, generate revenue and build customer loyalty by selling directly to consumers; second, improve profit margins by reducing transaction costs, primarily in marketing and distribution. Instead of sharing customers, now they began to compete for them.

Providers such as airlines and hotel companies sought to reduce reliance on fees to travel agents and Computer Reservations System (CRS) operators by selling directly to consumers through Web sites. In response to this threat to their cash flow, CRSs followed suit, reducing dependence on airline and agent transaction fees . The travel agents' response was to build online stores for leisure and business travelers. Credit card companies formed co-branded alliances with hotels and airlines to secure customer loyalty and supplier acceptance, and incorporated travel links into their online payment sites.

As a result, today's online travel market is highly competitive, but also reveals remnants of favoritism among providers and distributors, making consumer education critical. The evolution of the industry has renewed enthusiasm for government regulation.

Until standards exist - and in the online world, there are few but market forces - consumers who know how the various ticket-booking sites work can score bargains. However, in addition to demanding a certain level of expertise from consumers, airline ticket-booking sites also vary dramatically when it comes to matching bargain-basement fares with viable itineraries, good customer service, and strong privacy and security policies. .

Each site has advantages and disadvantages. Finding everything on one site can be challenging, but not impossible. It just depends on when and where you're going and when and where you book. Many of these challenges stem from the same issues faced by consumers in the traditional brick-and-mortar marketplace (for instance, one airline's fare getting promoted over another based on its superior position on a travel agent's computer screen). However, online technology can exacerbate these challenges, and can even obscure elements of transactions the consumer could more easily perceive in the "real world."

Consumers now have many more choices because the Internet gives more providers more opportunities to create direct consumer relationships and allows a wide variety of pricing. The good news is these choices afford more selection in terms of what, how, when and from whom to buy. But Web technology, coupled with the complex nature of the industry, has created an environment in which evaluating these choices can be mind-boggling.

The independent ticket-booking sites need to address basic disclosure issues - from describing how their technologies work to clearly disclosing business deals they make with airlines that might affect the price of fares, or their position on a screen. The six largest integrated travel web sites confirmed to Consumer Reports Travel Letter that they receive various forms of compensation from airlines, despite the fact most carriers have recently eliminated the payment of base commissions to travel agencies. Sites also should better separate airline and other advertising from screens of available fares, so the consumer is not manipulated into making a choice based on strategic placement of an ad. Fees should be more clearly disclosed, earlier in transactions - not at the end after a consumer has invested valuable time selecting a flight.

The Internet travel industry is approaching a crossroads. Until some form of standardization occurs, whether by regulation, market maturity, or both, shopping for the best travel deal online will continue to be confusing at minimum. At the worst extreme, the experience is a little bit like online casino gambling - experienced players can leave the table money ahead, but often, the house wins.

Computer Reservations System (CRS)

Deregulation meant that airlines that had previously

operated under government-set fares which ensured they at least broke even now needed to improve operational efficiency to compete in a free market. While there were many aspects to this, one of the earliest changes was the development of the Airline Reservations System (ARS), its evolution into and proliferation of the Computer Reservations System (CRS), and then into Global Distribution System (GDS).

The history of Airline reservations systems began in the late 1950s when American Airlines began to try to create a system that would allow real-time access to flight details in all of its offices, to integrate and automate its booking and ticketing processes. As a result, Sabre (Semi-Automated Business Research Environment) was developed and launched in 1964. Sabre's key breakthrough was its ability to keep inventory correct in real time, accessible to agents around the world. Prior to this, manual systems required centralized reservation centers, groups of human beings in a room with the physical "cards" that represented inventory (seats on airplanes).

This ability to keep all the data updated eventually led to the ability to price seats on airplanes at many different levels. Initially, however, since there were generally only three reservation classes per flight, sophisticated pricing strategies would have to wait. Other carriers soon followed with their own proprietary Airline Reservations Systems (ARS).

Quickly, a network concept emerged, which connected the various ARSs together and made them available to travel agents. This became known as the CRS concept. Just as the invention of the ARS enabled the automation of flight and seat control within an airline, the CRS concept automated the reservations process by placing the reservations technology for all airlines on a travel agent's desk, eliminating the need for the travel agent to call the airline to make reservations. This enabled the travel agent to spend more time helping the traveler and enabled the airline to, in essence, outsource the telephone reservation process. This saved the airlines millions of dollars, as the majority of the telephone-reservation work was transferred to the travel agent.

In 1974, an American Airlines executive, Robert Crandall, proposed that airlines jointly create, own and operate a large communication network with global reach for all travel agent offices, and prevent travel agents from taking full control of it. Unwilling to pursue that strategy without antitrust immunity, airlines instead accelerated development of ARSs by expanding them to include other providers and using them as distribution tools for travel agents. In 1976, United Airlines began installing its in-house Apollo CRS in travel agencies; American soon followed. Airlines were under cost pressure, answering calls from travel agents in direct contact with the customer, then inputting reservation information into their own internal systems. Call-center staff performing this work often were unionized. Thus, the airlines' strategy to put the computer and the reservation tools directly on the travel agent's desk outsourced a substantial cost.

What the ARS had done was basically automate the "old model" of a call center at which reservations were written on cards. The technology enabled this function to be distributed not only within an airline, but also to agents and independent businesses completely outside the airlines' control. Soon American's Sabre surpassed United's Apollo in market share and secured a dominant position. The success of the ARS and CRS was clear: In the late 1980s, Apollo's annual pre-tax return on investment had reached 70 percent; Sabre's was more than 100 percent.

Within the next 10 years, European airlines began developing their own CRSs. In 1987, two consortia were formed, and the European-based systems Amadeus and Galileo were designed much like the systems in the United

States. Amadeus was based on SystemOne that Texas Air's Frank Lorenzo acquired when he bought Eastern Air Lines. As one industry insider put it, "Frank had to take (money-losing) Eastern in order to get his hands on SystemOne, his real objective in the transaction." Galileo chose United's Apollo system as its strategic partner. In the Asia-Pacific Rim, CRSs primarily operated closely with national airline representatives, with the exception being Abacus, a consortium of Southeast Asian airlines' CRSs.

By the mid-to-late 1990s, the major CRSs essentially became GDSs that travel agents used to check real-time flight schedules, seat availability and pricing information, make bookings and issue tickets. The GDS operators collaborated with a variety of travel service providers such as airlines, cruise operators, hotels, railway companies and car rental companies, in addition to accepting special meal requests, managing seat allocation and performing back-office accounting functions for travel agents. At one point during this period, someone quipped that Sabre might be the most powerful non-military computer in the world.

By the mid-1990s, there were about a dozen major GDSs worldwide. Amadeus had become the world leader after merging with SystemOne, achieving a 27 percent market share; Galileo and Sabre followed, each with 22 percent. After these came Worldspan, formed by Delta, Northwest and TWA, with a 10 percent share, and Abacus and Infini, the dominant CRSs in Asia, with a combined share of 9 percent.

GDS technology developed with four functional components that, while integrated and interdependent, would later serve as points of differentiation when Internet providers entered the market and pulled apart the links of the supply chain. They were:

— inventory management and display;

— pricing- and fare-search engines;

— ticketing and document generators; and

— database reporting engines.

Inventory management and display comprised the systems that captured inventory (seats, hotel rooms, cars, etc.) of providers and, through sophisticated algorithms, displayed them on computer screens in response to an agent's keyed-in request. These algorithms were critical because of the physical limitation of the number of flights that could be shown on a CRS screen. Eighty to 90 percent of bookings are made using flights that appear on the first screen; an incredible 70 percent or more of bookings are made using the flight that appears on the first line of the first screen. This phenomenon, called screen position bias, raised regulatory concerns when the owner-operator of the reservation system listed their flights first. Travel agents tended to prefer reservation system owners who provided them with technical support and back-office systems, training and relationship management, causing further concerns. Airlines gave agents incentives to install their proprietary CRSs so they could get "first-line" position and thus generate more sales.

Pricing- and fare-search engines were sophisticated systems that would take an itinerary request and, based on a set of rules, determine the fare. The rules were a function of routings, stop-overs, advance purchases, length of stay and a myriad of other factors that, both fixed and variable, were essentially based on supply and demand. The infamous "Saturday night stay" rule was a key marketing tactic discovered by yield managers. It enabled airlines to assign a number of prices to the same itinerary because business travelers, spending company money, were very resistant to spending the weekend away from home.

Ticketing and document generators allowed agents to generate a physical or electronic ticket and also queue them to remote locations, such as an airport or out-of-state office, for pick-up. One creative use of this technology was when agents would queue tickets to remote locations for printing where the commission was higher, and then ship them back for actual delivery to customers.

Database reporting engines enabled airlines and agents to report transaction activity for a variety of purposes, including financial or accounting uses, trend analysis or passenger searches.

In addition, CRS technology required extensive communications networks to interface in a multitude of technical and geographic environments. Down time on a GDS meant lost revenue for providers, agents and the GDS, as well as frustrated travelers.

In time, more than 80 percent of airline tickets would be sold through CRSs by more than 130,000 travel agencies worldwide. Most of the remaining transactions, such as hotels and rental cars, were also booked through CRSs.

Money Flow

In the mid-1990s, the economics of travel were fairly straightforward: If a ticket cost $300, the revenue was divided so that the travel agent got about $30, the CRS $10, and the credit card company $6. The airline got the remaining $254, or about 85 percent.

If the same ticket cost $2,000, the CRS fees tended to remain the same, since they were generally segment-based - the example assumes $3.50 per segment for a 2-3 segment trip. Alternatively, the travel agent fee, based on a standard 10 percent commission, jumped to $200, for what many airlines argued was the same or less work if, for example, the higher-priced ticket was for a business traveler, who already knew which airline and flight he or she preferred. Disparities like this motivated the airlines to put pressure on travel agents, seeking changes in the compensation system and reduction of base commission levels.

Revenue Allocation

An airline's revenue varied according to the public's demand for travel - highly seasonal, elastic or price-sensitive for leisure travel, and more on-demand for business travel. The airlines' key revenue tool was the yield management system, which allowed them to sell the same seat for 15 to 20 different prices, depending on which market segment the traveler belonged to - business, leisure, price-sensitive, not price-sensitive, etc. They kept low fares from the business traveler by placing a requirement to either stay over Saturday nights or buy the ticket two weeks in advance for a cheaper price. They took what some argued to be a commodity, airline seats or hotel rooms, and priced them differently based on the trip's purpose, day, time, seat location and advance demand in order to maximize revenue. The primary pricing distinction was based on the purpose of the trip.

The travel agent's revenue was derived almost exclusively from commissions. In 1995, for example, agents were paid 10 percent of a domestic airline ticket's price, higher amounts for international tickets. To a lesser degree, hotels, transportation and cruise companies compensated travel agents, but these commissions were often difficult to collect as there was no proof the traveler actually stayed where he or she booked. Another important source of revenue, but hidden from the public's view, were supplemental "override" commissions, which airlines paid agents who demonstrated they could move traffic to premium levels, beyond an airline's "fair market share" on a particular route. These agreements are generally thought to have originated after the airlines outsourced reservations activity to travel agents. Doing this gave the agent much more control and "influence" in the traveler's carrier selection process. As override commissions could mean an additional 3 percent to 6 percent, agents were sometimes motivated to influence traveler preference toward the supplier that paid the most. For many agencies, overrides meant the difference between profit and loss, as base commissions were allocated to "covering the cost of operations" and the override "went to the bottom line." Consumer Reports Travel Letter studied the possible impact of these payments in June 2001.

Only about half the travel agencies surveyed immediately provided all the airline and pricing information, when asked, for the lowest-fare non-stop options on 12 different routes. This figure rose to 63 percent after the request was repeated, but 25 percent did not mention all lowest-fare options even after the second request. Furthermore, 12 percent did not provide lowest-fare options at all.

Charge card companies derived revenue by earning a percentage or discount fee of the face value of any transaction paid for with their card. This fee ranged from 2 percent to 4 percent of the transaction value depending on the merchant's volume of business. In addition to managing the receivable on the part of the supplier, credit and charge card companies promoted the benefits to customers and merchants: Convenience, security, information reporting and increased business.

CRSs' revenue came primarily from booking fees charged to airlines, and subscription fees paid by travel agencies and other subscribers to rent CRS terminals and receive technical support from the CRSs. CRSs segmented pricing strategies by region with transaction-based pricing dominating in North America, while net-segment based pricing was used outside North America. In North

America, in 1998, the cost-per-net-segment ranged from $3 to $3.50, plus a small fee for cancellations.

CRS Regulation

It is important to note that regulators became interested early on by Computer Reservations Systems and possible opportunities for abuse the technology created. Screen position bias, for example, was against free market principles and detrimental to fair competition. Since the CRSs were owned by the airlines and there were no legal restrictions on their administration, market abuses spread. New carriers complained of excessive fees to get their flights listed and established carriers complained of manipulated flight schedules, fare displays and searches. As a result, Congress launched an investigation in 1982, which confirmed the existence of screen position bias and other unfair practices. A comprehensive set of regulations were established in 1984, and then re-issued in 1992. They were designed to address the following four areas:

— *Displays* - Carrier-specific variables could not be used to rank flight primary displays. Secondary display bias was permitted under certain circumstances. Architectural restrictions, dealing with limiting flight searches, were allowed to continue.

— *Booking Fees* - Discrimination in fees charged to participants was prohibited. All participants were entitled to service enhancements.

— *Booking Data* - To the degree marketing data was developed, it had to be shared for a fee with all participants. In addition, owner carriers could not discriminate against other systems through "non-participation" in the other systems.

— *Agency Contract Terms* - Contractual terms with travel agents could not facilitate unfair competition. Agencies could use multiple systems.

Loopholes in these regulations did exist, particularly with respect to flight information display. Carriers would monitor competitive flight schedules and design their display algorithms so their flights would appear first. For example, if a carrier was being penalized by an elapsed-time algorithm tied to connections over a congested airport, the carrier might simply change the connecting time or flight time, sometimes to wildly unrealistic times in order to improve listing position.

Even stranger, carriers sometimes simply invented a new algorithm - say, the number of seats flowing over one connecting airport vs. another - that would serve the same purpose. In addition, CRS rules did not apply to non-U.S. airlines owning CRSs outside the United States. Although the objectives were shared, differences existed between U.S. and European rules. While the United States and Europe disagreed on CRS industry regulation, both maintained shared objectives and open communication. The continued bias in computerized reservation systems was one of two driving forces - the other being fees - that caused providers to seek alternative ways of distributing their products and services.

Within this broad economic framework, relationships between airlines and travel agencies, and airlines and GDSs, were not entirely mutually beneficial. Money was a zero-sum game and as one segment increased its profitability, another tended to suffer financially. From the providers' perspective, particularly airlines, the significant bookings handled by agents came at a high cost. Distribution costs were one of the airlines' top controllable expenses, up there with people, fuel, and aircraft ownership.

In 1997, a survey by the International Air Transport Association (IATA) indicated that CRS costs to airlines almost quadrupled in six years, from 2.1 percent of distribution costs in 1990 to 8.1 percent in 1996. And this was at a time when total U.S. distribution costs topped $18 billion. One U.S. carrier claimed its CRS cost increased 35 percent from 1993 to 1998, a period of relatively low inflation and declining technology prices. For the airline industry, distribution represented about 15 percent of the total costs in the late-1980s, and by 1990, was growing faster than passenger revenue.

By the mid-1990s, three important factors had gained enough momentum to drive the aggressive migration to and adoption of Internet-based travel: high distribution costs - and the obvious value-for-dollar question that was raised based on system bias; new technology that offered a cheaper alternative to GDS technology and direct access to customers; and a consumer population receptive and eager to take control of their own destinies.

Just as the airlines outsourced the labor-intensive process of researching and booking travel to travel agencies in the late-1970s, the Internet now provided them an opportunity to let the travelers do the work without the help of any airline employees or intermediaries, thus significantly lowering the airlines' costs once again.

TRAVEL ON THE WEB

The travel industry was one of the earliest to go online. Since travel had few geographical boundaries, and, thanks to the widespread adoption of e-tickets, which airlines aggressively pushed, the airlines faced none of the logistical issues of online product retailers such as shipping and variable tax-collection schemes, the travel industry was uniquely suited for the Web. As this report seeks to demonstrate, the lack of rules presented a major problem. There was no governing or marketing body to regulate rates, or online travel services that enabled consumers to efficiently navigate all the alternatives they had.

Bill Gates reportedly once quipped that Microsoft started Expedia because no other industry was as complex as travel, with so much constantly changing electronic information and consumers who wanted to become personally involved in the reservation-booking process.

With existing players and new entrants trying to capture a slice of the online market, new travel-related Web sites were springing up or reinventing themselves constantly. Many airlines, hotels, car rental companies, CRSs and national and municipal tourist organizations went online. Participants attempted to capitalize on the opportunity in travel by developing products aimed at attracting and retaining customers. To capture traveler loyalty, travel agents and CRSs built "consumer-friendly" front-end systems for existing information systems. They also leveraged relationships with emerging online service providers to work with business and leisure travelers in a cost-effective manner. In terms of size, complexity and sophistication, these first-generation efforts, by such players as EasySabre, Prodigy and ITN are far removed from today's mammoth sites.

Airlines reduced the need for intermediaries by offering direct-access software and encouraging business and leisure customers to purchase tickets directly from airlines. Each player in the travel supply chain would have its position challenged. Ability to adapt quickly would determine survival. In this new world, both the economics and even the players would change:

— Airlines reduced, and in some cases eliminated, costly intermediaries such as travel agents from their distribution chain. In 2001, there were 15 percent fewer travel agents in the United States than five years earlier. Airlines re-structured their distribution compensation agreements by segmenting them. Traditional transactions got one rate, electronic another. These categories were further segmented based on who, how and what was booked. In today's environment, travel agents provide less influence on carrier selection than they did in the past. Since the airlines no longer thought agents steered consumers to airlines, the airlines adjusted their compensation to virtually eliminate base commission payments in lieu of "pay-for-performance" structures. These pay-for-performance remnants of the "override" world continue to put financial pressure on travel agents' loyalties.

— Travel agents have redefined the way they charge consumers, in many cases unbundling their services. This may include charging a $25 service fee for issuing a ticket or a nominal fee for changing it. In the corporate travel arena, travel arrangers might pay for information management, on-site passport or back-office processing. Many travel agents invested in electronic servicing capabilities either independently or with technology partners, which had the two-fold objective of reducing their own service costs as well as providing entry into the new electronic market.

— Global Distribution System (GDSs) continued to consolidate and diversify their operations by unbundling their services and expanding their product offerings into other transaction-processing and information management services. These were meant to serve customers other than airlines, who were trying to reduce or eliminate GDS fees all together.

ONLINE TRAVEL MARKET

In 1997, Online Travel Market was estimated to have made up 1 percent of the total travel market. Today it has grown to 11 percent, valued at over $20 billion. The market was already growing prior to the terrorist attacks on New York's World Trade Center and the Pentagon in

Washington, D.C., on September 11, 2001, and since then consumers have continued to rely on these sites both as "looking" and as "booking" tools.

The demographic profiles of those who made online plans at the emergence of Internet travel in 1996 were more likely to be employed, educated to the postgraduate level and a professional or manager. Five years later, online travel has gained mainstream popularity, and there are thousands of sites that offer travel information and services. They range from direct providers (e.g. airlines, hotels, ground transportation) to support services (e.g. tour organizers, travel and trade publications, hotel management companies), tourism development organizations, eco-tourism coordinators and many more. Depending on the publisher, travel Web sites could be categorized as service providers, destination related or Internet travel agencies.

Online service providers are branded sites developed and operated by airlines, hotels and others that want to sell directly to consumers. These sites are similar to auto dealerships in that they focus on selling the products of a particular supplier - American Airlines, for example, will not direct a consumer to United for a lower fare or more convenient service. That means if you use a supplier's site and are concerned about price, you might have to shop around to get the best price among other supplier sites. For example, based on actual research, on one routing an airline site quoted the lowest fare as more than $1,200. A check on a travel agent's site for the same trip quoted a $400 fare on the same carrier, with a connection via a city along the non-stop flight path that could not even be found on the carrier's own site.

In early days, provider sites might only have offered information. Today, most offer a comprehensive array of products and services online. Major airline sites offer customers reservations, electronic tickets (e-tickets), seat selection, in-flight merchandise, reward points and sometimes discounted fares unavailable elsewhere. In addition, they may offer lodging, transportation-package deals and cruises through their alliance partners. For example, American Airlines offers and redeems AA miles when a member makes a purchase on AOL. Branded airline sites are currently the fastest-growing segment of online travel providers, up 26 percent in February 2001. The most popular site (as measured by most unique visitors) is Southwest Airlines. One reason Southwest is so popular is that it doesn't issue tickets, and historically travel agents could not book them via a CRS because Southwest refused to place its information on the systems. Today, Southwest's inventory is available online only at its own site. United and American are the largest airline sites in terms of sales.

Destination sites provide information and services about a country, city or area, including details on transportation, accommodations, sightseeing, dining and local cultural events. They may or may not offer advertising, online booking capabilities or discounts and coupons. Since destination marketing is usually the responsibility of the national or local tourism boards, their Web sites usually embody this tone. Their goal is to generate visits to the area, so they are less concerned with the mechanics of how the traveler chooses to get there.

Internet travel agencies are Web sites that expand traditional agents' offerings. In addition to selling regular travel services such as air tickets and hotel rooms, they also offer travel tips, destination information and other services. Many large traditional agencies such as American Express and Liberty Travel have extended their shops to the virtual marketplace. Consumer Reports Travel Letter in 2002 evaluated six of the largest and most well-known sites: CheapTickets, Expedia, OneTravel, Orbitz, TravelNow, and Travelocity.

Table 1. - Major Virtual Travel Agencies - 2002

Site Name	Customer Offering	Owner/Operator/Comments
CheapTickets	Multi-channel (online/offline) full service agency for discounted leisure travel products. Advertises one-stop shopping, electronic ticketing, personalization services, and low fare search technology, access to millions of published and unpublished fares.	- Founded in 1986 with a single retail store in Honolulu; acquired by Cendant Corporation in October 2001.
Expedia	Offers full service, online travel services for travelers and small businesses. Advertises one -stop shopping, "Best Fare Search", technological superiority. Suppliers include over 450 airlines, 65,000 properties plus packages and cruises.	- Launched by Microsoft in 1996; acquired Travelscape.com and VacationSpot.com in March 2000. - Partnership with USA Networks provides capital and resources for market expansion and new product development
OneTravel	Full service agency promoting economical leisure travel; offers air, car, hotel booking and ticketing. Advertises extensive supplier network 500 airlines, 54,000 hotels, 48 car companies, advice library and low fares proprietary "White Label" database and "Fare Beater" reservation system. Offers destination and weather information.	- Owner: Terra Lycos and Amadeus - Sponsor of Style World WE (Women's Entertainment Network)

Orbitz	- Full-service online agency; suppliers include 455 airlines, 210 hotel chains, 42 car companies 30 packagers and 18 cruise lines. Promotes site as ideal surf and buy site	- Full service agency promoting economical leisure travel; offers air, car, hotel booking and ticketing. Advertises extensive supplier network 500 airlines, 54,000 hotels, 48 car companies, advice library and low fares proprietary "White Label" database and "Fare Beater" reservation system. Offers destination and weather information.
TravelNow	- Discount Travel Booking service for air, hotel and ground transportation - promotes special discounts and deals on particular routes/properties.	- Owner: Hotels.com, majority owned by USA Interactive - Site is more like Web presence than e-commerce transaction processor; many transactions handled offline
Travelocity	- Full-service, online agency with extensive network of suppliers built by/ on top of Sabre CRS. Boasts Internet and wireless reservations information for more than 700 airlines, more than 55,000 hotels and more than 50 car rental companies, plus vacation packages, tour and cruises plus a database of destination and interest information. Features "Best Fare Finder" search technology, hotel mapping and concierge services.	- Sabre owns Travelocity.com and GetThere, a provider of Web-based travel reservation systems for corporations and travel suppliers. - Currently replacing management team after recent buyback by Sabre.

For consumers, online travel and its new world of self-service has brought convenience, access, speed and control. It has also brought confusion and lack of consistency - albeit a consistency once confining, but at least one that let a consumer identify a good deal or not. Now, customers whose experience with booking travel was traditionally insulated from the complexities that lay below the surface are now given more choices about how and where they book and more services from which to choose, and yes, pay for. One key theme in this latest evolution in travel has been a redefinition of who the customer is at each stage of the process, and aligning costs and revenues accordingly. In the old world, the customer paid nothing explicit for travel services. The cost of the service was bundled into the cost of the air ticket.

In today's environment, where the airlines have moved to zero commissions for travel agents, the cost of services - in the form of service fees - is now apparent. The airlines contend the consumer always paid for these services, but the money is no longer driving the airlines' financial statements.

Hence, leisure and business travel consumers have much more choice today in what and how they buy. It's not just selecting the destination, date, time, carrier and seat, but whether they want to research a trip independently or enlist an agent to help, receive an electronic or paper ticket, self-select the destination and travel logistics or have them selected for him based on excess inventory at deeply discounted prices. Today, travelers can tour hotel rooms through their Web browsers, find online references from other travelers and comparison shop in the most efficient way ever.

But given what we have discussed so far about how the air travel industry evolved in the last half of the 20th century, of the airlines' dominant role in all phases of its growth, and of how regulators in the 1980s felt compelled to establish rules where none before existed, what do consumers need to know about this new, fast-growing frontier in which the power appears to be in the hands of the people?

Consumer Experience

Consumer Reports Travel Letter last evaluated four large independent sites-Cheap Tickets, Expedia, Lowestfare and Travelocity-in October 2000. Though the findings were not conclusive, they did reveal some evidence travel sites may not always be totally objective:

— On Travelocity, advertised airlines dominated flight listings.

— On Lowestfare, many TWA flights with inconvenient itineraries were repeatedly listed first.

— On all four sites, certain airlines with viable itineraries for routes tested were not listed at all.

The concern about bias dates back to the 1980s, when the U.S. Department of Transportation (DOT) devised rules for Computer Reservations Systems after receiving complaints about biased displays from travel agencies and airlines. The DOT was clear about regulating only airline-owned CRSs, so that such systems couldn't unfairly aid their sister-company airlines.

None of the travel Web sites in this series of tests were owned by an airline, although all four accepted advertising. And in some cases, airlines pay for more prominent placement. Travelocity presents "featured airlines," which receive full-color advertisements linked to specific cities or airports. When you request a list of fares, Travelocity asks if you would like flights offered by the featured airline, or choices from other airlines, as well.

In Consumer Reports Travel Letter's 2000 testing, the featured airline on Travelocity was listed first 48 percent of the time and dominated other listings. In nine separate tests, each recording the top nine flight choices, the featured airline flew at least one leg of every trip that Travelocity posted. Many of these trips involved convoluted itineraries melded together with at least one other airline.

Lowestfare's contract agreement with TWA seems to have influenced its flight listings: In tests, that airline was listed as the first choice 50 percent of the time, when no other site listed TWA first more than 23 percent of the time. The TWA routings sometimes involved connecting flights when other Web sites offered non-stops.

Another concern was raised when cross-referencing test results revealed that certain airlines listed in the Apollo Galileo benchmark as offering the lowest fare and a viable itinerary were not listed on some Web sites at all. Spirit Airlines was missing from Expedia; Vanguard was absent from Expedia and Lowestfare; and Southwest appeared only on Travelocity, even though Cheap Tickets and Lowestfare receive data from Sabre, which includes Southwest.

A team of Consumer Reports Travel Letter and Consumer Reports WebWatch researchers asked these six sites for the lowest economy-class fares on 10 busy domestic non-stop routes throughout the United States. The itineraries included routes frequented by vacationers as well as business travelers. They sampled a variety of trips with advance bookings ranging in length from same day to 105 days. Nine simultaneous test sessions were conducted in all, at various times of the day and week, for a total of 540 flight queries, and the researchers recorded the first fares listed.

To establish benchmarks, the researchers simultaneously requested identical information from Sabre, the leading computer reservations system used by travel agents, but not available to consumers. Despite the influx of "Web-only" fares, we found that Sabre still provided a very strong benchmark. The U.S. Department of Transportation regulates Sabre and all other CRSs for fairness and accuracy in displaying fares and flights. Harrell Associates, a leading airline pricing consulting firm, processed the Sabre data for Consumer Reports Travel Letter.

It is important to note these results were based on the first displays returned by the sites. One of the reasons CRSs are regulated, as previously discussed in this report, is that it has been shown placement of fares is critical since, historically, travel agents have selected the "first fares." But the six Web sites offer more interactive screen displays than the CRSs do, and some other options offered further down the display were both low-priced and viable, when we searched for them. In particular, Orbitz offers users a wide variety of choices on its flight and fare screens.

In the October 2000 study, Consumer Reports Travel Letter raised concerns about some disturbing evidence of bias because tests showed a possible relationship between the airlines that advertised on those sites and the order in which flight choices were listed. These latest tests have once again raised serious questions about potential bias and the way flight information is displayed, and the waters have become even muddier. Since 2000, there has been an increase in the number of proprietary agreements between independent travel sites and airlines. The resulting Web-only fares have certainly brought great bargains to consumers. But it remains unclear how such deals have affected the ordering of flights and fares on these sites.

The agreements between independent sites and airlines and other travel providers are proprietary. But all six of these sites confirmed to Consumer Reports Travel

Letter that they receive various forms of compensation from airlines, despite the fact most U.S. carriers have recently eliminated payment of base commissions to travel agencies. For example, Travelocity stated it has "reached broad marketing agreements with several airlines" and "receives compensation for the value and services it provides the carrier, including e-mail campaigns, promotions, sweepstakes, and banner advertising." Airlines traditionally pay incentive commissions to agencies - online or offline - in order to increase market share.

Consumer Reports Travel Letter was interested to see what happened when a smaller carrier operated the lowest-fare flight offered in Sabre. This is particularly important for Orbitz, given its controversial ownership by major carriers American, Continental, Delta, Northwest, and United. In the spring of 2002, key members of Congress were asking the U.S. Department of Justice to examine Orbitz for potential antitrust violations, particularly because the site receives guaranteed lowest fares from its owners on many routes - fares not routinely available to other travel sites. This followed the launch in April of a review of Orbitz by the Inspector General of the DOT.

The result was that in the 18 cases in which Sabre's first pick was a small carrier, Orbitz offered a higher fare in 11 cases, or 61 percent of the time; the other five sites offered a higher fare from 5 percent to 50 percent of the time. However, in these cases CRTL did not see a pattern of Orbitz favoring major carriers over smaller competitors.

Are such omissions or reordering of fares the quirks of a complex pricing mechanism or examples of bias? It's impossible to know. But it is fair to say that-even overlooking the issue of ownership - the relationships between Web sites and their airline advertising and marketing partners have raised reasonable doubts in both

the studies. The DOT recently announced another extension, in addition to numerous previous extensions, of its review of the CRS regulations, so federal oversight of online travel commerce does not appear to be imminent.

VIABILITY OF FLIGHTS

As price remains the most important feature for online travel shoppers, this was the key criterion of the research, however saving $25 while adding 10 hours and 2 stops to your trip is usually not a choice many travelers would readily accept. To determine flight viability, Consumer Reports Travel Letter looked at:

— A single-airline itinerary.

— A departure time no more than one hour prior to that requested.

— A departure time of no more than four hours later than that requested.

— No more than one connecting flight, but non-stop flights preferred.

— A connecting time of no more than three hours.

— A connecting airport no more than 700 miles from a straight-line route between origin and destination.

In the 2000 study, most sites provided an attractive ticket price as a first choice, but sometimes with very impractical itineraries. The best sites then provided viable itineraries about half the time. Two years later, the two best sites provided viable itineraries 55 percent to 60 percent of the time - better, but still far short of Sabre at 98 percent. Expedia in particular didn't seem to listen when an evening departure time was requested.

For example, Expedia listed as a first offering an Atlanta-Miami departure at 7:30 a.m. when researchers requested a departure at 6 p.m. In fact, in 11 separate cases,

Expedia's first offering was at least 10 hours earlier or later than the requested departure time. Expedia's connecting flights also strained credibility at times. For example, a round-trip from Atlanta to Miami included stops in Dallas on the departing flight and Washington, D.C., on the return. Another Atlanta-Miami trip included stops in Charlotte on the departure and Newark on the return.

Consumer Reports Travel Letter determined five elements key to navigating an integrated travel site:

— Broaden or narrow airport search parameters.
— Specify the number of stops en route.
— Select a seat.
— Modify the flight information mid-search.
— Re-sort search results by price, departure time, or total flight time.

In both the 2000 and 2002 studies, the top sites far outperformed the second-tier sites in this area. The top sites are investing more in customer interface and user-friendliness, while some of the second-tier sites are holding steadfast in their niche - such as CheapTickets, which has restricted search capabilities and advance purchase requirements.

In evaluating customer service of online travel Web sites, Consumer Reports Travel Letter looked at several criteria:

— Toll-free numbers and availability of customer service help
— Email responsiveness
— Cancellation/refund policies
— Change Fees

While the sites vary in their customer service capability, the top sites again edged out the smaller sites - particularly in the 2002 study. It's clear the smaller sites are vying for a niche market, while the largest ones are clamoring for dominance. This can be good news for consumers, provided they are aware of the trade-offs.

CURRENT INTERNET TRAVEL CONCERNS

The concerns fall into two broad areas: Industry issues and consumer issues. Industry issues involve the proverbial clash of titans - the major travel players, providers, CRS distributors and travel agents. Consumer issues focus on the plight of individual travelers - system functionality, ease of use, reliability of results, and the most important consumer concern, getting the best transportation at the best time at the most reasonable price.

The industry titans are each pointing out the bad things the other is doing. As a result, there are currently about half a dozen cases where members of the group are urging the U.S. government to regulate some other member. This report's goal in this very complicated situation is to fairly present all sides of the major players' main issues in an easy-to-understand way.

Airlines believe that it costs too much to distribute their product and are pressuring CRSs and travel agents to reduce costs. Considering the travel agent community is very disaggregated, with tens of thousands of agents, airlines began by reducing base commissions paid to travel agents. They began in the mid-1990s and had just completed the final round when base commissions were reduced to zero. Agency compensation actually continues under the guise of pay-for-performance incentives and override payments designed to reward agents for providing premium market share for airlines.

Airlines have also developed their own booking sites on the Internet to facilitate direct bookings, and are luring travelers to these sites with "Web-only" fares, i.e., very low fares available only at their Web site. In addition, the major U.S. airlines have established their own Internet travel agent, Orbitz, designed to circumvent travel agents and CRSs, though Orbitz currently depends on a CRS for much of its functionality. Orbitz has been given "most favored nation" access to low Web-only fares, and is using that facility to grow its business from a start-up in the middle of 2001 to the third-largest non-airline Internet booking facility one year later. These fares were initially thought of and criticized for being exclusive.

Now it appears the arrangement is not exclusive, as other Web sites and some brick-and-mortar stores are also getting these fares, either from the airlines directly or via Orbitz itself. Airlines reason that it is the net fare that matters, and they should be free to offer their lowest net fare (Web fare) on a selective basis. If this means offering these fares only through the distribution channel that does not further dilute that low fare, then so be it. Airlines also believe that CRSs abuse their dominant market position and should be investigated by the government.

CRSs believe their costs provide good value, and challenge anyone to develop a better mousetrap than Amadeus, Galileo, Sabre or Worldspan, in which they have invested millions of programming hours to develop. They think their product, while perhaps not the perfect distribution machine, provides an efficient solution for the most complex and demanding electronic business in the world. They vigorously support Internet travel agents that use CRSs, such as Travelocity and Expedia. They don't like the airlines' complaints about high costs, and believe that the airlines' creation of Orbitz is an abuse of market power and should be investigated by the government.

Travel agents are furious that the airlines have reduced their commissions and are angry that they created Orbitz to bypass them. They believe the government should investigate the airlines and Orbitz. In fact, they also support a government investigation of themselves, to show how much they contribute to the industry. At press time, this investigation, originally mandated two years ago and funded in October 2000, was set to get underway in mid-June, 2002, with a mandate to report back in the middle of November 2002. The investigation will have a broad scope and will include both brick-and-mortar agencies and Internet agencies. Travel agents also create uncertainty in this complicated mixture - some might say havoc - through incentive agreements with the airlines providing compensation for shelf position in the office, on the phone, and most recently, on the Internet.

Some say it's analogous to the supermarket contest for premium shelf space involving Wheaties vs. Cheerios. This time, however, it's being played out on the Internet as airline flights and fares suddenly disappear from the screen as commissions` are cut and other "marketing arrangements" remain unconsummated. For example, earlier this year it was widely reported one major airline had its screen position adversely changed after it reduced commissions and did not promptly offset this action with other marketing arrangements. Also, Consumer Reports documented a case in which a major carrier withdrew its seats from an agent that it didn't think was properly marketing the airline's flights. Agents retort that they should not be forced to represent providers that do not compensate them for their services, especially if the marketplace is not willing to do so in the form of service fees.

Consumer issues mostly concern the booking process and include such issues as ease-of-use, reliability of results, and most importantly, the best price and value. First, know that good, and sometimes great, deals can be made through online travel sites. Remember that providers want repeat business. Patience and flexibility can go a long way. Surf when shopping for travel online. Take the time to look at different sites and return a few days later. Also, remember the "law of diminishing returns."

Tips for Buying Tickets Online

Here's some advice when using online travel sites, whether booking or just looking:

— Compare airfare results on several different Web sites to find the best deal. Remember that bookings are in "real-time" and can change rapidly. Expedia and Travelocity allow users to create an itinerary and hold the reservation. Although they don't guarantee price, you can return to the reservation later if you decide to book the flight.

— Make sure you understand the site's fee structure. Neither Expedia nor Travelocity charges a flat fee for transactions, regardless of the airline. However, such fees often vary based on the airline's agreement with the site - these deals are nearly always in flux. Just because one site charges a fee for a given airline doesn't mean all will.

— Check the rules before you buy: refundability and reusability, transferability and upgradeability. Find out if your "great" deal allows you to accrue frequent flier mileage or if there are any "hidden concessions."

— Be flexible. Often a lower fare is available if you're willing or able to choose alternate travel dates, flight times or airports. Many large cities have secondary airports nearby. Also, connecting flights, while adding time, can also save money as long as the routing and extra time invested is reasonable.

— There can be a difference between the price of an e-ticket and the price of a paper ticket, particularly if you book online. If you choose to have a paper ticket sent to you, be aware it is likely to come with an additional charge.

— If you're using a travel agency, let the agent know about the deal you've found online and see if the agent can beat it. Inquire about the agency's preferred-supplier deals with specific airlines, and ask if those agreements can provide any benefits.

— Once you find a low airfare on a specific airline, go to that carrier's own Web site and see if you can find an even lower fare.

— If Southwest flies the route on which you're planning to travel, visit its site to compare your search results, since it is the only major carrier that doesn't display its fares and schedules on any of the agency Web sites. Southwest's fares can rarely be beat.

— If you're flexible on your travel dates and times, consider using one of the Web sites that allows booking of deeply-discounted and completely nonrefundable airline tickets.

— Some sites include airline advertisements on their search pages. Don't let them confuse you. Be sure to view all the available options.

— Whenever possible, book your airline ticket several weeks in advance. You'll have a better chance of securing low-priced seats that often sell out first.

6

SELF-BOOKING OF FLIGHT TICKETS

A decade ago, when e-commerce was a relatively new phenomenon, which was seen as a revolution in business practices, it was commonly predicted that e-commerce was set for a fast and tremendous growth, and that the travel industry, which has been identified as a sector highly suitable for e-commerce would become one of the first industries to be transformed by technology and to experience disintermediation due to the emergence of Internet-based distribution channels.

In spite of high Internet adoption rate among the general public and the constantly growing number of online transactions made, the volume of e-commerce has not, although showing a fast and continuing increase, been able to meet the early predictions of analysts, industry experts, and practitioners who came to overestimate the promise of e-commerce. Disappointing figures, typically heavy losses from their Internet operations, have forced many companies, especially Internet start-ups to re-evaluate, revise, or terminate their more or less failed Internet strategies.

It has been suggested that the somewhat disappointing e-commerce growth figures reflect the fact that the online services, systems and interfaces offered in the early years of e-commerce were not advanced enough to generate true customer value and drive consumers towards Internet commerce. Accordingly, it seems reasonable to assume that ecommerce has a significantly greater growth potential as such limitations are overcome and the online services have matured and improved.

Today there is little doubt that the expectations on Internet commerce were, initially, too optimistic. Although the beginning of this millennium showed, as a result, post-euphoric and exaggerated cynicism towards IT and e-commerce, the vast commercial prospects of the Internet are still acknowledged by scholars, governments and businesses, and we are seeing signs that the Internet indeed will have a great impact on the global marketplace, but that the path has been - and will be - evolutionary rather than revolutionary.

In the last few years, there has clearly been an ambition to base the Web-based services and e-business models on the customers' mindset and expectations rather than on technological hype. In this respect, an interesting issue is: Have the online services improved and matured, and have greater prerequisites for successful e-commerce been implemented as both service providers and customers have gained more experience with e-commerce?

Looking into the travel industry, arguably one of the most interesting industries in terms of the use of IT and e-commerce, this chapter aims to explore whether, and to what extent, online reservation services have improved and evolved in the last few years - especially as far as high-complexity travel arrangements are concerned. This is done by replicating a small-scale empirical study conducted almost seven years ago.

E-TRAVEL

The travel industry, one of the largest and fastest growing industries in the world, has appeared particularly interesting in terms of the possibilities offered by IT and e-commerce. Overall, the travel industry has been a forerunner in terms of using IT, with, immense global distribution systems (GDSs) emerging already several decades ago. Theoretically, the presumed suitability of the travel industry for electronic commerce can be explained by the high information intensity of the tourist product.

The fact that tourism, at the point of sale, is little more than an information product has thrust it into the forefront of the electronic commerce revolution. Information can largely be conceived as constituting the tourism product since it is characteristically intangible, perishable, volatile and heterogeneous.

Since information - in particular real-time information is the foundation on which the travel industry is built, the potential for value-adding (online) electronic services is immense.

Indeed, the Internet has the potential to offer a great number of advantages not only to industry players, but also - and especially - to consumers. In the context of travel and tourism, a number of potential benefits stand out as especially relevant. Of these benefits, the one listed last (price reductions) has received the most attention in the e-commerce literature.

— A tool for joint holiday decision-making

— Greater amounts of multimedia destination information

— real-time information on price and availability.

— Control of the search for information, allowing them to feel sure that all of the available options for their trip have been investigated.

— The Internet empowers even tiny tourism organizations and destinations, giving them representation in the electronic marketplace, thus providing consumers with a wider selection of travel service providers

— Time savings resulting from the rapidity of purchasing process

— The ease of bookings as the travel reservationmaking process can be automated by Internet technologies

— Price reductions resulting from increased competition as more suppliers are able to compete in an electronically open marketplace, as a result of reduced selling prices due to a reduction in operational/ transaction costs, and manufacturers internalizing activities traditionally performed by intermediaries.

DISINTERMEDIATION

Watson et al. contend that the Web will change distribution like no other environmental force since the industrial revolution. Not only will it modify many of the assumptions on which distribution channel structures are based, but in many cases it will transform and even obliterate channels themselves. In doing so, it will render many intermediaries obsolete, while simultaneously creating new channels and, indeed, new intermediaries. This assertion summarizes, in brief, a topic that has gathered widespread attention among scholars and managers engaged in e-commerce, namely disintermediation, which can be defined as the reduction or elimination of the role of retailers, distributors, brokers, and other middlemen in transactions between the producer and the customer.

The information-intensive travel industry has been seen as especially interesting in terms of bypass threats, as it is an outstanding example of a sector where the position of the intermediaries - the travel agencies - traditionally has been strong although they have, paradoxically, been seen as an unnecessary overhead by the suppliers. According to Licata et al., it is evident that the Internet has started a process of change in the travel product buying habits of both leisure and business users.

The disintermediation phenomenon has been subject of numerous studies since the mid-1990s. Although much of this work has been conceptual in nature, a few empirical studies on the plausibility of the disintermediation hypothesis have nevertheless been documented. In general, the opinions and research findings on the matter have been conflicting. Early predictions were that e-commerce would create efficiencies by eliminating the need for intermediaries, but in later research many scholars having taken a different stance in the disintermediation debate, either rejecting the disintermediation hypothesis altogether, or - more typically - predicting different development paths, suggesting that the need for intermediaries is not likely to be eliminated in the near future. Instead, it is often argued that

(i)   some of the traditional roles of middlemen may at most, change or become less important as a result of advances in IT;

(ii)   that cybermediaries (new entrants with intermediary functions) will gain a strong position on electronic markets, or

(iii) that online subsidiaries of traditional middlemen will be able to reintermediate in the long run as EC-able intermediaries.

As is the case with the disintermediation hypothesis in general, opinions also tend to differ on the plausibility of disintermediation in the context of the travel industry, which has been hypothesized to be among the first sectors to experience disintermediation on a large scale as a result of Internet commerce. Most commentators would probably agree that the pre-Internet position of travel agents is unsustainable, and that travel agents that fail to take advantage of the Internet are faced with a real threat - at least in the long run.

Yet, there is little empirical evidence to support any arguments and predictions relating to the future role of middlemen in the travel distribution chain: Drawing on data from surveys of managers and travel consultants of Australian travel agencies, Standing et al. and Vasudavan and Standing forecasted that many high street retail travel agents will be eliminated over the next few years. Using data collected through the Delphi method, McCubbrey predicted that major disintermediation and cybermediation will occur and that there will be a sharp reduction in the number of traditional travel agents five and ten years in the future.

Based on an exploratory survey among industry experts, Licata et al. forecasted that more conventional forms of distribution, i.e. global distribution systems (GDSs) and high street shops, are likely to be bypassed, or that their roles will change dramatically. Anckar used consumer survey data revealing an intention by a significantly growing number of consumers to abandon high street travel agencies, also showing that the emergence of travel reservation services through mobile electronic channels is likely to reinforce and expedite the disintermediation phenomenon by attracting a large portion of the many non-shopping Internet users to the electronic marketplace.

The main argument for rejecting the disintermediation hypothesis has been a conviction that middlemen, either new entrants or established players who launch operations online, will continue to have a strong position in the electronic marketplace. Although each of the scenarios presented; disintermediation, reintermediation, or cybermediation have different implications in terms of the future role of middlemen, they are, nevertheless, closely related.

Table 1. Potential problems associated with consumer online travel reservations

---

— Technical problems, systems limitations, or poor online services / site usability

— Difficulties finding online service providers and/or locating Web sites (due to the enormous

— size of the Web, there may be a need for some previous knowledge of where to look)

— Complexity of international flights and GDSs (may lead to incorrect bookings)

— The uncertainty factor: Is the itinerary possible/convenient? Is the fare reasonable? Are the ticket restrictions acceptable? May lead to hesitancy to book online.

— The time consuming nature of the task (high search costs)

— Poor knowledge about low-fare booking strategies, rules and restrictions, etc (may lead to expensive fares and greater risks - such as nonrefundable tickets).

— The availability issue: Services/tickets matching the traveler's schedule or preferences are not necessarily available.

— Difficulties coordinating services and schedules poor coordination of journey components

— One-stop shopping not possible. Often not possible to book travel directly online or to buy the separate parts of a trip through the same supplier.

— No access to travel agent negotiated rates (leads to expensive fares)

While disintermediation points towards an elimination or reduction of intermediaries altogether due to direct producer-consumer relationships, cybermediation is an equally detrimental outcome for traditional high street players, who are replaced by new middlemen drawing on IT-enabled business models.

Reintermediation, on the other hand, secures the position of traditional middlemen, but only for players that are able and willing to renew their operations and establish value-adding online services. Consequently, all of these electronic scenarios for middlemen are likely to alter distribution chains by eliminating intermediaries strictly operating with established business models. Thus, the opposite position to disintermediation is continued intermediation, a nontransformation of current industry structures, which means that the emergence of electronic channels will not have significant transformational effects on the distribution chain.

The seemingly good suitability of travel products for e-commerce suggests that consumers embracing ecommerce within this sector will obtain many important benefits, especially when using selfbooking online services, and that the threat of disintermediation may be real as a consequence. Intuitively there seem to be, however, several potential hindrances to a mass-market adoption of direct consumer-to-producer electronic shopping solutions in the context of travel and tourism. According to Sheldon, consumers, surprisingly, have the potential to experience more disadvantages than advantages by using online travel services.

EMPIRICAL STUDY ON THE EFFICACY OF SELF-BOOKING

To identify and to assess the magnitude of a number of potential problem areasin the Internet booking process Pirkko Walden and Bill Anckar conducted an exploratory study in December 1998. The study was conducted among 24 students attending an intermediary level course on ecommerce, data were collected using two different exploratory research techniques: First, an uncontrolled field experiment (an Internet booking task) was conducted in which the students, acting as travel agents, were to submit a detailed offer for a high-complexity, multi-destination journey according to given specifications.

The students were instructed to submit an offer of a round-trip from Turku, Finland to Maui, Hawaii for two persons. According to the instructions given, the travelers were to set out on the journey on January 2nd in the early morning (local time). The students were allowed to use their own judgment when planning the route. However, a booking comprising more than 8 intermediate landings during the journey (there and back) was considered unacceptable. An additional requirement was that none of the intermediate landings would last longer than 5 hours - with one exception: The travelers wanted to rest by putting up at a hotel for one night on both routes. All accommodation facilities (two single rooms) during the journey were to be high-class (the students were given detailed instructions). During the visit, the travelers also wanted to make a day's journey to the island of Kauai. The students were instructed to submit an offer on this excursion as well. The travelers wanted to be back in Turku on January 15th in the morning (local time).

The students were given 14 days to complete the task under instructions that all bookings were to be made over the Internet. Hence, they were not allowed to pay a visit to a travel agency or to contact one by phone or fax. Correspondence over e-mail with Webbased travel agents was, however, acceptable, but this possibility was deliberately not emphasized when the students received their instructions, as an interesting aspect of the task was to see which approach the students would consider and choose. The task was announced as a quotation competition, and the student who obtained the lowest price was later awarded a prize. No student or regular customer discounts were allowed.

In order to investigate the problems encountered when completing the task, the students were asked to fill in a self-administered questionnaire. The questions covered the potential problem areas mentioned in the previous chapter and the chosen approach to solving the task. In the questionnaire, the suggested impediments to smooth Internet-bookings were investigated by presenting some statements to which the respondents were to express the magnitude of their agreement (1 = strongly disagree, 4 = disagree, 3 = neutral, 4 agree, 5 = strongly agree).

The results of the study were surprising, suggesting that even experienced Internet users have difficulties producing satisfactory travel arrangements online, while also revealing significant perceived barriers to using online travel reservation services. Especially the great range of variation in price was surprising. The task was completed by 23 students, however with very varying results: The price difference between the highest ($ 19.587) and the lowest ($ 5810) offer was as much as $ 13.777, or 337.1 %. In spite of clear instructions, as many as 14 of the 23 students did not make the bookings according to the given - and strict - instructions. A total of 4 students managed to submit an offer lower than the one made by the travel agency ($ 7364), but only one of the students managed to undercut the price offered by the travel agency as far as the flights tickets were concerned.

The initial study was later followed up by three further exploratory studies in 1999-2000, the aim of which were to test four hypotheses that relate to the intuitively realistic supposition that low-complexity travel arrangements are better suited for direct distribution over the Internet than high-complexity arrangements. The follow-up studies, which involved booking tasks classified as rather straightforward, were conducted in a similar manner as the initial experiment. Surprisingly, the results of these studies confirmed that even booking tasks that are to be seen as rather low in complexity can prove to be highly problematic for the average online booker.

When reporting on the findings from the study from 1998, Pirkko Walden and Bill Anckar contended that a key issue in terms of e-travel is whether we will see a further development of the online reservation systems in the future, eliminating the travel agencies' current advantages in speed, knowledge and intuition. They argued that the results indicated a strong belief among the respondents in more advanced reservation systems and improved consumer terms in the future. Based on that postulation as well as on the common, and intuitively reasonable assumption that the online systems and services will improve with time, they decided to repeat the first study seven years later, in 2005.

The study was completed in an almost identical manner as the first study. The basic task was nearly identical, but some minor modifications were nevertheless made: The Island of Kauai was set as the destination instead of Maui, and the journey dates were slightly different - primarily due to the fact that most of the (American) online booking sites do not allow reservations to be made more than 330 days in advance. Moreover, no quotations were taken from a professional travel agent. Again, the study consisted of two parts: (i) a quotation competition in which the students were to act as travel agents, submitting an offer for the journey according to the given specifications; and (ii) a self-administered questionnaire, in which the students were asked to report on the problems encountered when completing the task. In order to get a better view of the problems involved in the booking process, a few items were added to the original questionnaire.

In addition, the students were instructed to keep an online diary, in which they were to report on problems, opportunities, experiences, and actions taken during the task, and to write a brief report on their booking experiences. The study was conducted in February 2005 among a sample of 15 students taking part in an intermediary level course on e-commerce. The students were given 3 weeks to complete the task as an uncontrolled experiment. All quotations and prices had to be documented. In addition, the task was given to another group of students, who were to complete the task as a classroom experiment in two hours. However, none of the students managed to submit an offer for the entire journey in that time, a result which shows the complexity involved in the task.

Nearly all of the 15 students (12 males, 3 females) making up the sample considered themselves to be proficient Internet users; (somewhat proficient: 26.7%; proficient: 33.3%, very proficient: 40%). All the respondents (100%) reported that they visit the Internet every day. The mean age of the sample was 24.4 years. In 2005, the completion rate was 100%. In 1998, the corresponding rate was 73.9%.

All the submitted offers are a sum of the two travelers' total travel arrangements and are stated in US dollars. In 2005, the price difference between the highest ($ 8368.65) and the lowest offer ($ 5253.95) was 59.3%, or in other words much less than in the 1998 study (337.1%). The average quotation amounted to $ 7363.00 in the 2005 study, whereas it was $ 11382.00 in 1998. In the 1998 study, it was necessary to adjust the initial offered prices somewhat, since the students had left out some specific component of the travel (or booked it incorrectly), making the offer incomplete. In 2005 the problems were minor, such as not observing the different currencies used in the quotations. In both studies the price was adjusted, where needed, by adding a sum roughly equivalent to the average offered rate for the specific component to the total price.

On the whole the participants in the 2005 study completed the task according to the given requirements, yet using very different strategies: Some students had discovered the possibility to book a packaged tour (including flights, hotels and the rented car) from New York or Los Angeles to Kauai. This caused, of course, problems (as well as inaccuracies) in estimating the price of certain components in the packaged tour.

On an average, the students spent 6.40 hours on the task in 1998, but significantly more time (15.65 hours) in 2005. In 2005, the participants in the study contacted more service providers during the task, but used online reservation sites almost exclusively. 40% of the students chose to send e-mails to travel agents (in 1998 the corresponding figure was 37.5%), but on an average they sent only 0.6 message each (against 4 messages each in 1998).

In the questionnaire, the students were also asked to report on their satisfaction with their performance in the task. In 1998, 39.1% of the students were either extremely satisfied or satisfied, whereas 30.4% were dissatisfied or extremely dissatisfied with their performance. When asked if they intended to make their travel reservations over the Internet in the future, it seemed to be the case that most students had not formed a strong opinion based on the experiences of the assignment: 3 students responded yes, 5 no, and 15 perhaps.

In 2005, only 33.3% of the respondents were satisfied with their performance in the task. Still, 80% reported that they likely or definitely will make their travel reservations over the Internet (only one responded unlikely): 46.7% reported that they probably will book the trips themselves through selfbooking sites, whereas 33.3 are likely to use both online travel sites and Web-based travel agents and compare prices.

The students were also asked if they thought that they could have been offered a better price by contacting a travel agent for this particular task. Most respondents were unsure (53.3%), but as many as 40% responded likely or yes, definitely.

Problem Areas

As far as the general difficulty of the task is concerned, 43.5% of the respondents found the task difficult in 1998, whereas 46.71% agreed or strongly agreed to the same statement in 2005. As the greatest impediment to the bookings was - as in the 1998 study - cited the *time-consuming* nature of self-bookings, and it is important to note that the ratings were even much higher in the 2005 study.

Another major problem area - with significantly higher ratings in 2005 than in 1998 - was making price comparisons. This finding is in line with (and partly explained by) the fact that self-bookings are perceived as time-consuming, but the problems involved in making price comparisons also emerge from the constantly changing availability situation and online fares, and the frustration this may cause the self-booker.

The study from 1998 showed that even experienced Internet users have difficulties producing satisfactory travel arrangements online, while also revealing significant barriers to using online travel reservation services. In the first study from 1998, the most striking result was the huge range of variation in the price of the online bookings completed. Overall, the data collected in the 2005 study largely reinforced the findings from the 1998 study, indicating that many problems and limitations are involved in the online travel booking process from the consumer's point of view, especially as far as highcomplexity arrangements are concerned.

Obviously experienced Internet users seem to have fewer difficulties producing satisfactory travel arrangements online in 2005 than in 1998. The price variation was significantly lower than in the previous study, and the bookings were, as a rule, made correctly.

Completing a satisfactory high-complexity reservation online appears to require massive efforts in terms of the time spent online. On a general level, it appears to be much easier to find travel service providers online today than in 1998. Likewise, the results indicate that the overall usability of the sites has improved, and that fewer technical problems occur. It thus appears to be the case that greater prerequisites for successful ecommerce have been implemented, probably as both service providers and customers have gained more experience with Internet commerce. Still, many students complained about the user-unfriendly interfaces on many web sites, which also were seen to be lacking in functionality.

Although some barriers to self-bookings are shrinking or disappearing, the information abundance on the web - with an increasing number of sites and service providers - seems to be creating new barriers in terms of the time and efforts required to produce satisfactory travel arrangements online. Without further technological advances and reliable rate finders, these barriers are likely to remain and even grow in the near future. Likewise, the growing number of online service providers is likely to emphasize the uncertainty factor (in terms of assessing the "right" fare for a certain journey), thus causing hesitancy among consumers to book online.

The data collected in the study rendered contradictory scenarios in terms of the plausibility of the disintermediation phenomenon: On one hand, (i) the rather high perceived barriers, (ii) the students' dissatisfaction with the outcome in light of (iii) the activities undertaken during the booking task would, rationally, inhibit the movement toward direct distribution. On the other hand, as many as 80% of the students reported, while affirming the difficulty of self-bookings, an intention to use online reservation services when making their travel arrangements in the future.

Observing these outspoken intentions, the study supported the vision of disintermediation - at least as far as the role of traditional travel agents (human assistance) is concerned. The inconsistency of the two indicators on this matter may suggest that consumers, in spite of the considerable practical hindrances to using the online booking services, recognize the obvious and potential advantages offered by electronic travel services in comparison to traditional distribution methods. Moreover, it may imply a confidence in more advanced reservation systems and improved consumer terms in the future. Nevertheless, the potential significance of the observed barriers with regard to a widespread adoption of online travel services should not be underestimated.

7

E-COMMERCE AND AIR TRAVEL DISTRIBUTION

The computer reservations systems (CRSs) developed for the travel industry were among the earliest examples of e-commerce. Forty years ago American Airlines developed the Sabre computer reservation system to keep track of seat availability on hundreds of flights for thousands of passengers booked all over the world. Airlines have continuously expanded their use of information technology for reservations systems and created an infrastructure that facilitates the application of OR models.

The Sabre system and similar reservations systems, such as Amadeus, Galileo, Shares, and Worldspan, have transformed the travel industry. They have improved product distribution and customer service, and have revolutionized airline marketing through yield management and frequent-flyer programs. These reservation systems have evolved into global distribution systems (GDSs). Where CRSs helped individual airlines sell and manage their own seats, the GDS consolidates information from many airlines, allowing travel agents, businesses, and individuals to shop in a single electronic marketplace. This marketplace has expanded to include hotel, rental car, and destination products and services.

The growth of reservation systems and the related use of OR in the airline industry have parallels in the evolving world of Internet-based e-commerce. As noted in *Forbes* online, "Sabre was an early version of an electronic marketplace, fashionably called an infomediary. . . The similarities between Sabre and the new infomediaries are quite stark. Infomediaries are web-based market makers that leverage the Internet to bring together buyers and sellers in niche markets, charging commissions for the products they help move. . . Sabre-type infomediaries took in $290 million in 1998. By 2002, . . . that number will grow to $20 billion." As stated by Phillips, "Global distribution systems brought the airlines to the electronic marketplace a quarter century before the rest of us."

By consolidating product information from many airline suppliers, global distribution systems created a marketplace with close-to-perfect information regarding schedules and fares. Using the Internet, other industries are converging towards a similar scenario by adopting such functions as low-price search engines, display ordering- rules logic, and real-time technology that the airlines pioneered. The airlines built up their e-commerce infrastructure over 70 years, and the history of that evolution provides insights into current changes in other industries. History of Airline E-Commerce In the prejet commercial era, a few hundred passenger airliners carried just a million passengers per year.

In the 1950s, the introduction of commercialjet engines, cabin pressurization, and improved navigational aids revolutionized air travel. As demand increased, airlines developed internal communications and commercial infrastructure to coordinate the activities of staff, aircraft, and passengers.

SITA (Socie´te´Internationale de Te´le´communications Ae´ronautiques) and ARINC (AeronauticalRadio Inc.) were among the world's first business-to-business systems. They used Teletype messaging for communicating electronically among the airlines. SITA and ARINC are still used today. They employ message pass-through capabilities the airlines developed to transmit information on passengers' travel itineraries and payments. Many businesses have the same communication needs that drove the airlines to develop SITA and ARINC, but costs and technical requirements prevented their developing customized systems. This unmet business need made low-cost communications through email one of the first killer applications of the Internet.

Two of the most difficult information- processing problems the airlines faced were

(1) keeping track of the number of seats sold on a growing number of flights and

(2) communicating remaining seat availability to geographically dispersed reservation agents.

The manual solutions developed in the 1930s were difficult to scale up as the airlines grew. For example, the size of reservation offices was limited by the feasible distance between agents and a chalkboard used to track sold-out flights. At one point, some American Airlines agents used binoculars to read flight availability.

Airlines tried to solve the problem using available technology; the solutions tended to be expensive and barely adequate. In 1953, American Airlines and IBM began working together on the problem. After five years, they formed a partnership to develop the first CRS. In 1962, they implemented the Sabre system for American Airlines' production use. Design, development, and implementation took 400 labour years. It was the first realtime business application of computer technology, an automated system with complete passenger records available electronically to any agent connected to the Sabre system. At that time, American Airlines processed an average of 26,000 passenger-reservation transactions per day and the average time to file a reservation decreased from 45 minutes to three seconds. This jump in efficiency allowed airlines to handle the growth in demand for air travel that occurred in the 1960s.

Through the 1970s, the CivilAeronautics Board (CAB) regulated domestic airfares in the United States. Discount fares were not widely available on scheduled carriers except for narrowly defined demographic groups, such as children and students. Cheaper air travel was available only on unscheduled charter carriers. By the mid-1970s, some chartered carriers started to operate quasi-scheduled flights. Relaxing regulations, the CAB allowed these low-cost carriers to begin competing in the scheduled airline market. Their high costs put the scheduled carriers at a disadvantage.

They realized that every empty seat .own was produced at almost zero incremental cost and selling otherwise empty seats at low prices could increase revenue and profits. Initially, they restricted discount fares heavily in an attempt to segment the market and avoid diluting the existing business-fare revenue. Today they still employ some of the initial restrictions, such as advance purchase, round trip, and Saturday-night stay. To fill otherwise empty seats, the airlines increased the number and diversity of discount fares.

Airlines developed yield management to fine-tune their increasingly complex pricing structures by tracking reservations and selectively turning on and off the availability of low fares. Yield management applies operations research models to determine the appropriate amount of space to save for late-booking high-revenue customers. The combination of pricing restrictions and yield-management controls allowed carriers to offer very low fares with little risk of diluting revenues. This was critical for airlines serving both high-revenue business customers and price-sensitive discretionary customers.

Following US airline deregulation in 1978, airlines that controlled their inventories with yield management generated much higher profits than those that did not. A notable illustration is the experience of PeopleExpress. It started service in 1981 and within five years became the fifth largest airline in the United States. At that time, PeopleExpress was the fastest growing company in US history. It could offer low fares because of its no-frills service and nonunionized labour. It had load factors of about 75 percent while the rest of the industry had load factors around 55 percent.

In January 1985, American Airlines launched a discount-pricing campaign, "Ultimate Super Savers," directed at filling the otherwise empty seats. It offered full service at discount fares priced at or below low-cost carriers. It used purchase restrictions and yield-management-based inventory control to prevent the displacement of future full-fare sales by early-arriving discount-fare demand. The overwhelming demand for discount fares and full service shifted traffic to American Airlines and other carriers using similar practices.

PeopleExpress load factors dropped to around 25 percent; the airline was sold to Continentalin September 1986. According to Donald Burr, former chairman of PeopleExpress, "We were a vibrant, profitable company from 1981 to 1985, and then we tipped right over into losing $50 million a month. . .What changed was American's ability to do widespread yield management in every one of our markets. . ."

As passenger volumes increased in the early 1970s, the paper-intensive processes travel agents used proved too slow. They needed automation to print itineraries, invoices, and tickets, and to handle accounting. In 1974, an effort called the Joint Industry Computer Reservation System (JICRS) was launched to provide automation to travel agents by creating one reservation system for all airlines. Airline participants included American, United, TWA, Eastern, and Western. The plan was to develop a system to display and book reservations on any airline, accommodating the need of travel agents to offer industry-wide travel products and services.

JICRS was one of the first industry alliances to undertake e-market efforts. The JICRS effort was disbanded in 1976, when United Airlines announced plans to install its own proprietary system, Apollo, in travel-agent locations. Airlines that owned and operated CRSs rushed to expand their capabilities (to display information for multiple airlines) and to install their systems at travel agencies. The urgency was based on the value associated with display bias.

Agents who subscribed to a given carrier's reservation system were provided with flight information biased towards that carrier. For any travel request, many flight alternatives generally exist, even if the traveller has specific preferences (for example, a narrow range of departure or arrival times). The algorithm the GDS used to identify potential itineraries considers schedule convenience (proximity to desired departure time, number of stops, elapsed time) as well as the carrier(s) providing the service. Flights for the carrier operating the GDS were sorted higher in the list of candidate itineraries.

The order in which itineraries are presented on the travel-agent screen has a powerful impact on the traveller's choice. All things considered equal, the first few choices presented have a higher likelihood of being selected. Copeland, Mason, and McKenney cited findings that an average of 70 percent of all bookings were made from the first screen display (the first six options) presented to a travel agent. By the mid-80s, the incremental revenue associated with display bias for American Airlines was estimated at over $100 million per year.

GDSs (such as Sabre) became the gateway for information about all airlines to the travel agent. Control of travel product distribution by a handful of carriers put many airlines at a disadvantage. In November 1984, the Department of Transportation (DOT) regulated several key functions of reservation systems to eliminate bias in their displays. The rulings required unbiased displays of flights; public disclosure of display rules by the GDSs; standardization of the timing of daily fare changes (to prevent a carrier from unfairly showing a special fare in its own reservation-system before competitors had the opportunity to load their fares); providing reservation-system booking data to all airlines (possibly at a charge); and charging equal booking fees. Ironically, the electronic marketplace that had been energized by the deregulation of US airlines was regulated within five years.

INTERNET AND TRAVEL DISTRIBUTION

Prior to the Internet, airlines, GDSs, and travel agents communicated across private networks. Public networks supporting the Internet significantly reduced the cost and complexity of communications between the airlines, GDSs, travel agents, and end consumers. Early Internet reservation applications were limited to booking and payment transactions only.

Paper tickets were mailed to the travellers, and they had to make purchases seven days in advance if they were to receive their tickets in time to travel. Electronic ticketing facilitated the growth of Internet travel sales by eliminating the need for paper tickets, reducing the lead time and cost associated with online purchases. According to Forrester

Research, 9 million households booked travel reservations online in 1999. By 2003, this number is expected to surge to 26 million, and another 16 million households will research travel online. On the corporate travel front, Forrester projects a revenue volume of $38 billion in 2003.

Internet ticket sales have grown rapidly because distribution methods are tailored to customer needs. Three models dominate the Internet distribution channel:

(1) online travel agents (such as Travelocity. com and Expedia) provide direct GDS access to travellers;

(2) airline web sites provide direct links between airlines and customers;

(3) auction and reverse auction outlets bypass the traditional distribution network and act as mediators between suppliers and customers.

Online travel agents, such as Travelocity. com, allow customers to search for travel itineraries that best suit their personal preferences through price-driven and time-driven searches. Customers can also specify additional preference parameters, such as number of connections and airline. Responding to customers' requests requires more resources in the GDS than responding to travel agents' requests.

While the Internet has spawned a variety of multisupplier distribution models, it has also revived the airline sales agent in electronic form. Many carriers use the Internet to attract and retain customers by providing additional services such as realtime flight and airport information, online management of frequent flyers, auctions for popular destinations, and online vacation packages. The Internet is also being used to notify known potential travellers about the reduced fares on distressed inventory.

Carriers are offering special promotions, such as exclusive reduced fares and increased mileage, to encourage bookings through their Web sites. Some airlines are also restricting promotions to members of their frequent-flyer programs. For example, Delta offers "more for your miles" auctions in which members of their frequent-flyer program can bid their accumulated miles on vacation packages. Airlines are using operations research tools, such as demand forecasting and optimization, to design sales promotions and to identify cross-selling opportunities, such as rentalcar, hotel, and other destination interests.

They can use customer-profile data captured from the users' navigational paths while browsing the Web (their clickstreams) and other customer-related data as input to identify promotion opportunities, tailored to individual customers. For example, an airline in contact with someone wanting a seat on a completely booked fight might be able to transfer that demand to another flight leaving around the same time or from a nearby airport by emailing an offer (flight, price, restrictions) instead of a refusal. Carriers are also using the Internet to cut distribution costs.

While the industry sold two percent of all tickets through airline Web sites in 1999, Southwest Airlines sold 15 percent of its tickets through its own Web site. Outlet such as LastMinuteTravel.com are based on concepts of distressed inventory and dynamic pricing. They mar down unsold inventory close to departure and advertis it on the Internet.

Customers shopping at this type of outlet must willing to adapt their travel arrangements to the mark quality (in this case, in the form of traveltime and locati convenience) is sacrificed for price. The success of th sites (the profit for auction hosts) depends on the cho of sale timing and price. Early discounting (before airline realizes the regular demand for its flig completely) may result in revenue cannibalization for airline. Insufficient markdown of fares might not stimulate enough demand. The sites interact with the airlines' revenue-management systems seamlessly to determine when and how many seats to auction.

Auction outlets, such as Priceline.com, collect bids from travellers and match them with product offerings from participating airlines. As the customer must accept (within certain parameters) any product that meets the specified price, auction models cater to travellers who have decided to purchase and who are willing to sacrifice quality for price.   ·

The auction host's profit is the difference between a customer's bid and the price of the matched product offering. An auction host may opt to accept losing bids to increase revenue. When evaluating a customer bid, the auction host faces the same basic problem as online agents. Hence, the host can use techniques similar to the ones described for the online agent to find cheap fares. If the auction host has access to demand and fare-availability forecasts, it can use yield management to increase its profit margin.

The Internet is creating opportunities for air travel beyond the traditional scheduled airlines. For example, the Internet is enabling charter operators to compete effectively for business travel. Flightserv.com is an online marketplace for charter-business-jet travel. It plans to allow customers to create and book their own routes. Once a customer books a new route, that route will be offered to other potential travellers over the Internet. If successful, this will improve the efficiency of jet charter operations to levels comparable to those of scheduled airlines.

DECISION SUPPORT IN AIRLINE MARKETING

The e-commerce infrastructure the airlines developed allows collection and central storage of sales and marketing data. Airlines use this data to drive decision support tools for planning and marketing.

Airline Planning

Decision-support models for airline planning are generally directed at estimating the demand, revenue, and cost of proposed schedules. After studies revealed the large impact of GDS screen presence on customer choices, airlines have tried to increase demand by improving their screen presence by adjusting their schedules. They make small adjustments to improve screen presence, such as

(1) determining which origin-destination markets will be served by through flights as opposed to connections in a hub and

(2) reducing (or increasing) scheduled flight durations to improve screen presence (and increase demand) at the expense of on time dependability.

Airlines also have modified the fundamental nature of their product offerings to improve screen presence by

(1) making agreements with partner airlines to assign multiple-carrier codes to the same flight so that interline connections will be displayed as single airline connections or one-stop through flights and

(2) by creating funnel flights by assigning multiple flights the same numbers so that connections will be displayed as one-stop through flights. While many considered these practices deceptive, they became industry standards as airlines pursued screen presence.

The tasks of estimating demand and determining appropriate schedule adjustments are daunting. Airlines developed CRS simulation models to estimate screen presence and the resulting market share. Airlines that owned GDSs used CRS simulations to determine the display parameters that most favoured their schedules.

Given these published GDS parameters, other airlines used CRS simulations to improve their screen presence. Market-share models are calibrated using market information data or customer-information data that contain booking information.

Customer-information data consist of protocols of randomly selected sales sessions that occur during the booking process. These data are analogous to clickstream data and are used to calibrate discrete customer-choice models typically based on multinomial logit or nested logit approaches. Customer information data are, in general, regarded as the best data source for building passenger-preference models based on screen presence.

The market-share estimates produced by CRS simulation models are essential parts of airline profitability analyses. Airlines use the market-share estimates in several stages of the schedule-design process to determine the basic schedule structure, service frequency, and timing. Once an airline establishes the base schedule, it uses a fleet-assignment model to assign aircraft types to flights.

The objective of this model is to maximize captured revenue minus operating cost while meeting various operational constraints. The primary input to the fleet-assignment model for estimating demand and revenue comes from the airline-profitability model. Currently the airlines manually develop the base schedules and input them to the fleet assignment model. Several efforts are under way to develop decision support for this initial step of schedule design.

Display regulations governing the traditional GDSs do not apply to the Internet-based distribution channels. Online travel agents and auction outlets can establish their own display rules. To date, airlines have not taken advantage of the Internet to develop new processes for scheduling flights. In the future, we expect that airlines will collect data corresponding to the Internet-based demand and then design a schedule that best accommodates this demand, or auction space on provisional flights and operate the schedules that will collectively produce the greatest profit. So far, no major carriers have announced such plans.

Other industries that distribute products through Internet channels have product planning problems similar to those the airlines faced. They need models to track product visibility, to adjust products to the channels, and to estimate the impact on demand and revenue. If privacy issues are resolved, detailed customer-shopping information will become widely available. Firms will likely use discrete-choice modelling to estimate market share and product demand. Firms, such as Amazon.com, are using collaborative filtering and similar techniques to personalize Web-site content by predicting individualpreferences based on the navigational paths of customers considered to have similar tastes.

Airline Marketing

The most important modelling application in airline marketing is yield management. American Airlines benefited by $1.2 billion over a three-year period from its yield-management practices. Yield-management systems use historical flight-demand and passenger booking data to set reservation-availability controls.

Airlines typically use several types of models in these systems. They use forecasting models to predict future demand and cancellations and base three types of decisions on these forecasts: flight overbooking, discount-fare management, and itinerary control. They use overbooking models to determine the maximum number of reservations (generally more than physical capacity) to accept. They use fare- management models to determine when to stop selling discount fares to avoid losing later-booking, higher-valued sales. They use traffic models to determine the best mix of long-haul (usually connecting) and short-haul (local) passengers. The contention for seats caused by multiple origin destinations flowing over the same flights, combined with multiple fares for each origin-destination pair, and the uncertainty of underlying demand requires a stochastic optimization approach to yield management.

Airlines generate additional revenue by carrying freight on passenger flights and by operating separate freighters; in 1998 Lufthansa made $1.331 billion (17 percent of total revenue) by shipping air cargo. Following the success of yield-management practices in passenger business, airlines devised similar techniques to improve the profitability in air-cargo business; Cathay Pacific Cargo estimated that its revenues increased 3.8 percent in the fourth quarter of 1996 because of yield management. Sabre developed a cargo-routing guide that finds alternative routes that meet the requested service and shipment characteristics. Airlines use the cargorouting algorithm when they compute the yield-management controls and when they respond to online customer requests.

When airlines set yield-management controls, they use the routing model to identify alternative routings for each market and service level. The yield-management controls are computed by considering the combined capacities of all routing alternatives. When responding to customer requests, airlines use the routing algorithm to find the cheapest feasible route.

The routing problem is solved by using a shortest-path algorithm with side constraints. The algorithm generates a hierarchical decomposition of the flight network. A modified bidirectional Dijkstra-type algorithm uses the decomposed network to respond to online routing requests.

Internet distribution has changed the yield-management problem drastically. As airlines sell their excess inventory through Internet auctions and other outlets, they are extending yield-management practices to include dynamic pricing and focused targeting of discounted fares and promotions to individuals. The new channels enable airlines to capture previously unobserved portions of the price-demand curve; the demand associated with low fares (auction and unpublished fares).

This is changing the airline pricing structure from oligopoly (whereby airlines publish their fares via a single forum, the Airline Tariff Publishing Company) to retail (where each airline sets up its own fare products). This focused marketing is affecting the forecasting and optimization algorithms airlines use to compute yield management controls, because these fares are lower in value and in cancellation risk.

Airline decision-support systems were extended to other travel-related industries. Sabre and SNCF (the French national rail - road, Societe´ Nationale des Chemins de Fer Franc,aise) jointly developed a schedule-planning system to determine fleet mix and configuration, service frequency, timing, and railcar routing for high-speed railservice. Derivatives of the airline profitability model, the fleet-assignment model, and the fleet-routing model have all been applied to the passenger-rail business.

Unlike airlines, SNCF publishes schedules for only 80 percent of its high-speed capacity. It schedules the remaining 20 percent during the final 14 days prior to departure based on the strength of advanced booking. This flexibility allows SNCF to closely match supply to demand. Sabre and SNCF jointly developed a model to assign and route this incremental capacity in the network to maximize profit. Researchers have advocated this procedure of adjusting capacity close to departure for many years, and airlines, such as Continental, are now attempting to make it a practice. Sabre has also helped Amtrak, SNCF high-speed trains, and Eurostar (the channel-tunnel high-speed service) develop yield-management processes. The hotel and cruise industries have also adopted yield-management systems, using forecasting, overbooking, and price management.

Hotels can benefit by determining the best mix of one-night versus multiple-night reservations. The problem is similar to that of determining the best mix of short-haulversus long-haul reservations for airlines, so hotels can rely on corresponding models. Since hotels and cruise lines can have many different room (or cabin) types, customer upgrades add another dimension of optimization complexity. While these applications of scheduling and yield management are closely related to the airline experience, the Internet has made yield-management modelling practical for a much wider range of industries, such as broadcasting, retail, manufacturing, and power generation.

Karaesmen and van Ryzin describe the analogies between yield management in travel and transportation and inventory and production theory. The random yield in inventory and production is similar to the number of reservations remaining after cancellations. The allocation of manufacturing capacity and inventory to various product demands is identical to determining availability controls for various travel itineraries. Despite these similarities, there is a major difference.

The capacity in travel and transportation is fixed, while the capacity in manufacturing tends to be flexible. Goodwin et al. extended the concepts of yield management to business-to-business exchanges in the manufacturing environment. They developed a distributed decision-support framework to match the capacity and demand across multiple suppliers and consumers using the Internet search engines and yield-management models.

Priceline.com has extended the potential application of yield management even further by creating a business model that can support yield management of home mortgages, new car sales, long-distance-calling minutes, and groceries.

While it is not clear to what extent Priceline.com practices yield management, the potential clearly exists. Without the Internet, none of these industries could have developed the infrastructure or critical mass of consumers to support this type of flexible marketplace. The wide applicability of yield management and its value to both consumers and suppliers may make it one of the next killer applications of the Internet.

TRAVEL DISTRIBUTION MODELLING

A large number of processing resources within the GDS are required to respond to shopping requests, that is, finding the best flight itineraries and fares based on travel agent or consumer requests. For example, about 50 percent of Sabre's CPU resources are dedicated to this function.

Sabre, like the other major GDSs, stores data in a schedule-oriented way. While this provides for very efficient schedule and itinerary searches, it does not promote efficient price-driven searches. The volume of price-driven requests, which initially increased following airline deregulation, has skyrocketed following the introduction of the Internet channels directed at bargain seeking consumers. The number of price driven requests the Sabre system handles has approximately doubled each year for the past three years. The search strategies used in Sabre that evolved fairly slowly between 1980 and 1997 required major retooling to keep up with the requirements of Travelocity.com and other growing channels.

In 1984, Sabre developed the Bargain Finder, which takes a customer's itinerary as input, performs an extensive fare search, checks fare rules, and returns the cheapest fare-class combination for that itinerary. Despite its limited functionality, Bargain Finder proved very valuable to travel agents because fare rules are complex and hard to check.

In 1993, Sabre developed an enhanced version called Bargain Finder Plus, which considers alternative fare classes on the given itinerary and alternative flights. It uses a two-step heuristic. In the first step, it uses local fares to select a set of alternative flights for each portion of the itinerary. In the second step, it generates and ranks a subset of all combinations of the previously selected flights. It displays the best itineraries.

Bargain Finder Plus was very well received by its users and quickly became a widely used tool in Sabre. However, because the two-phase heuristic performed extensive, complex fare-rule checking to establish valid fares for single flights and itineraries, running Bargain Finder Plus took more of Sabre's CPU resources than anticipated. In addition, many of the itineraries Bargain Finder Plus produced had very similar characteristics. Often, alternatives differed by only a few dollars or by minor differences in departure time, leaving the user with few real alternatives.

In 1997, Walker proposed a dynamic-programming algorithm using marginal utilities to improve Bargain Finder Plus performance. In the revised model, flight utilities are based on such characteristics as number of stops, airline, total travel time, and timeliness. The algorithm builds itineraries with maximum marginal utility and produces itineraries with the desired diversity. Moreover, it greatly reduced CPU usage, saving Sabre about $6 million per year.

With the advent of Travelocity.com and related sites, the need for tools like Bar- gain Finder Plus increased dramatically. Prior to Travelocity.com, travel agents were the only users of Bargain Finder Plus. They typically used Bargain Finder Plus to perform fine-tuning at the end of the booking process. Customers booking over the Internet more frequently rely on low-fare search tools as their main information sources, so efficient algorithms that support low-fare searches are essential for Travelocity.com and other online agents.

An ideal search algorithm uses a customer-specific preference profile to construct a utility function addressing service and fare and efficiently finds itineraries that maximize this utility function. Since the customers' utility functions are unknown (often even to themselves), the goal of the search algorithm is to produce a diverse set of options that has a high likelihood of containing an acceptable (if not the optimal) itinerary.

From a modelling perspective, Travelocity. com and related sites face a k-shortest (least-cost) path problem with side constraints. They need to find a feasible set of routes that best fits the selected utility function. Problem size, complex fare rules, and dynamic data make the instances that arise in the context of low-fare search particularly hard to solve. For example, a customer wants to book a round trip from New York City (NYC) to Los Angeles (LAX). For any given departure date, there are over 2,000 fare-flight combinations for each way of the round trip on 12 airlines providing service. That number increases if we include interline connections, where a passenger changes airlines along the way.

Moreover, the fares filed for an origin-destination pair can be undercut by using other stations as connection points. With six additional connection points, the network will contain over 5 million paths from NYC to LAX. Each path represents a combination of fare and itinerary. This example shows the importance of eliminating dominated paths early in the search process, especially since the problem has to be solved multiple times per second. Discount fares are restricted by complex fare rules that make it hard to identify feasible paths in the network. Some rules specify valid travel dates, advance purchase requirements, or minimum-stay restrictions. Others, so-called combinability rules, restrict fare combinations. The first type of rule can be checked when the fare is selecte while the latter must be checked when each path constructed.

Sabre developed a shortest-path algorithm that us data aggregation and bounding techniques to limit tl search space. The algorithm builds a search tree using tl departure station as root node. Each node of the tree associated with a partial itinerary. In each iteration, tl algorithm uses data aggregation to establish a lower bound on completing a partial itinerary. At this stage, it evaluates fare rules that restrict fare combinations to make bounds as tight as possible.

It considers the actual node costs plus the lower bound on completion cost when expanding the search tree. A shortest-path approach to the low fare- search problem gives users such information as the cheapest possible fare to complete the requested route along with conditions that need to be satisfied to get this fare. Other modes of transportation, lodging, and rental-car options can be included in the search as well. Hence, the shortest-path algorithm can be used to build customized vacation packages.

Moreover, it can be used to choose from a pool of prepackaged vacations. Search engines similar to Sabre's Bargain Finder Plus operate using the data available in other GDSs; Best Buy Quote, Power Pricing, and Seven Day Search operate on Apollo/Galileo, Worldspan, and Amadeus, respectively. Unlike these search engines, ITA Software's pricing tool bypasses the GDSs and works directly with data on the airlines' published and private fares and rules. The ITA search engine sifts efficiently through over a billion fare and flight combinations for each travel request. The specific techniques employed in these search engines are not published in the literature because of the confidential nature of the subject.

TRAVEL DISTRIBUTION REGULATION

Many early travel Web sites were at least partially owned by airlines, and new ones are planned. For example, a consortium of major carriers is collaborating on a new travel Web site, Orbitz. Unless the carriers clearly state that the site is airline owned, Orbitz customers could be misled into thinking that they are getting a complete and unbiased range of alternatives. The US Department of Justice is investigating whether Orbitz is anticompetitive. Regardless of the outcome of the investigation, the self-regulation driven by market forces will probably have a large impact on the neutrality of airline-owned reservation sites. These market forces will ultimately promote the neutrality of sites operated by multiple suppliers.

Even in genuinely neutral infomediaries, bias in some form is unavoidable for technical and commercial reasons. First, any system will require rules that determine what to display. The factors affecting the display ordering of competing alternatives can be weighted. For example, connecting flights can be given less weight than direct services, interline connections can be penalized compared to single-carrier connections, and multistop flights can be disadvantaged compared to nonstop flights. By analyzing the displays that result from different weighting combinations, one can develop selection rules that favour one carrier over another. Second, common business practices, such as suppliers (airlines) offering volume-based commissions, create powerful incentives for Web sites to promote certain carriers over others.

The airlines' rush in the 1970s to penetrate travel agencies with new automation tools has a clear parallel to the Internet economy. While airlines developed automated distribution tools for their own benefit, Internet distribution is an industry in its own right. Portals and search engines derive their value by providing access to many products and services. It is not uncommon for portals to contain exclusive links to service providers and e-retailers.

For example, MSN.com links to a single travel-service provider, Expedia; and America Online has agreed that Travelocity.com will be its exclusive travel-service link. Priceline.com gives Delta priority treatment. Unlike other suppliers, Priceline.com uses only highest qualifying fares to fill requests on Delta. Also Delta is entitled to revenue sharing, has the right to approve new airline participants, and may prevent Priceline.com from serving some markets.

The technical and commercial issues airlines and GDSs face are those any infomediary displaying goods and services of multiple vendors (such as mortgages, insurance, and personal computers) must face. Generally infomediaries must make money. Suppliers are paying for two things:

(1) inclusion on the Web site and

(2) prominent display.

Display bias invites government regulation. In assessing bias, one must decide whether users view the Web site as an extension of the supplier. Customers expect a company's own Web site to be biased. For example, Dell or Micron wants to sell its own personal computers.

However, if customers view the Web site as a public utility (that is, as a neutralsite), bias can be insidious. The airlines have learned to tailor their products (flight schedules and airfares) to different distribution channels (originally the major GDS vendors and now the Internet) to maximize their screen presence and sales effectiveness. Other companies doing business on the Internet must consider the screen presence of their products (relative to those of their competitors) on the leading Web sites. Companies can use decision-support tools to assess product visibility and channel presence, so as with the airlines, suppliers that fail to do so will be at a competitive disadvantage.

OPERATIONS RESEARCH

The success of airline applications and the communications, data, and control afforded by the Internet are encouraging other industries to apply decision-support models. The Wall Street Journal summarized the situation: "Eventually, many suppliers are likely to use the Web's fine-tuned interactivity to perfect yield management strategies similar to the way airline tickets are priced today, slashing prices to avoid surplus inventory or to quickly respond to changes in customer preferences".

The evolution of OR models for the airlines provides valuable guidance to the application of modelling to new industries facilitated by the Internet. Both depend on

(1) the availability of data to support planning and marketing decisions;

(2) suppliers' control of price and product availability; and

(3) dynamic "storefronts" provided by infomediaries who control product visibility.

Since the airlines started developing their models, however, the pace of change has quickened. Potential applications for forecasting, pricing, yield management, scheduling, and resource allocation arise almost daily. Development time has been reduced. This reduction in the development time will put OR modelling on the critical path with greater frequency. As a result, we must develop models faster. We must use high-level modelling languages and tools for this environment.

The pressure to develop applications rapidly and the high expectations associated with them are raising the risks and the rewards for OR modelling. Even the most successful model s don't get it right every time, and many don't get it right the first time. An optimization related glitch was estimated to have cost American Airlines about $50 million in 1988. We are seeing similar high-profile problems in some other applications.

Because it underestimated demand, the Encyclopedia Britannica Web site failed to serve most of the customer requests during its launch. Because it greatly overestimated demand, Williams-Sonoma, an upscale kitchenware and home-furnishing retailer, was left with 40- percent higher post-holiday inventory levels than in the previous year. In this evolving environment, OR practitioners need to respond to extreme pressures to cut the time to market but ensure that they take enough time to maintain reliability and credibility. This is particularly true when decisions involve multiple components, such as forecasting, optimization, and delivery.

Some modelling issues have not changed. Data availability and quality is often the most constraining aspect of an OR project. The data associated with new e-commerce applications may be cleaner than those from legacy systems; however, these data are often used along with data from the existing systems. Combining and cross-referencing data from multiple applications often highlights errors in each data source and inconsistencies between sources.

It seems unlikely that data from the Internet will take less time and effort to verify. Second, successful modelling approaches should include provisions for measuring their benefits. Unfortunately, the modelling task to measure benefits is often as challenging as the task of developing the model to be measured. Performance measurement can have major impact. For example, Sabre has worked on major reservation-system developments justified solely by the incremental revenues obtained from yield management. Performance measurement will continue to be essential.

Finally, as business processes change rapidly, models will likely have shorter life cycles. This may appear problematic, because businesses have less time to benefit from successful models. But they may also benefit. It has always been difficult to maintain the core mathematical model s in decision-support systems over the long term. Integer programming expert Ellis Johnson coined the term model petrification to refer to the organization's loss of understanding of models after the original development team departs. As responsibility for the models passes from team to team, the organization gradually loses insight into the models. Often it can no longer enhance or adapt the models to changing business requirements.

8

INTERNET AND AIR TRAVEL INFORMATION CONTROL

Historically, airlines have been treated as a special industry by the government. The reasons for this special treatment are multi-fold.

1. Airlines evolved from government subsidized airmail carriers.

2. Airlines have always been perceived as a ready reserve of military transport.

3. Airline pilots are also viewed as a ready reserve of pilots for the military.

4. Airlines are a symbol of wealth and power both at home and abroad, and are considered to be an effective means of "showing the flag" overseas.

5. Airlines exist as one element of continued economic development in almost all states.

AIRLINE BUSINESS

Two different business philosophies exist in airline industry. One is premium pricing and the other is discount pricing. Premium pricing is practiced by the large hub-and-spoke airlines while discount pricing is a philosophy of airlines such as Southwest. The fundamental underlying principle dictates how the airline collects and chooses to use information. In premium pricing, an airline attempts to maximize profit for each seat sold. This means the airline attempts to obtain the highest possible price possible for all seats. Since it is not possible to get all consumers to pay top dollar for every seat, airlines then must begin to lower the cost of a seat, or groups of seats, until each seat is sold.

In this manner, the airline has achieved ideal yield management where it has obtained the highest dollar amount from each customer possible for each seat sold. This type of yield management is highly information dependent since the airline needs to know the maximum amount of information about each customer possible to determine the maximum each customer is willing to pay to fly between two locations.

In discount pricing, instead of trying to determine how much revenue they can obtain from each aircraft seat, the authority determines what the minimum amount they can charge per seat while still maintaining a profit. This is called as the Wal-Mart pricing plan where the company always seeks new ways to sell products/seats at a lower price. In order to continue to discount prices, the company expands operations and improves efficiencies.

Information is also critical for a Wal-Mart pricing strategy, but focuses less on the maximum the consumer is willing to pay and more on the potential market for any given city pair if the price of an airline seat drops below a certain level. Likewise, with the Wal-Mart pricing plan, Southwest must constantly examine its own overall cost structure to ensure that the airline offers the lowest ticket prices possible. This philosophy is exemplified by Southwest Airlines' gradual expansion, even after September 11, 2001, as well at its low cost per seat mile-

constantly one of the lowest in the industry. Each business philosophy, premium pricing and discount pricing, influences many strategic airline decisions including how each distribute their tickets.

IT AND AIRLINES

Airlines are the second most dependent industry on information technologies, the first being the financial industry. Because of its dependence, airlines are quick to adopt new technologies to improve efficiencies that are expected to translate into cost savings. This dependence is exemplified by the airlines adoption of early mainframe computing, the creation of the CRSs/GDSs, Web ticketing, and eticketing. The fact that airlines are uniquely dependent on information collection, processing and distribution cannot be emphasized enough when examining airline strategy.

Please realize that "unbiased" or "neutral" technologies DO NOT exist. Technologies are created, used and manipulated by biased people and leveraged for specific purposes. Some airline will be listed at the top of the screen; someone's banner will be run as an ad. Given this reality, any other technology that multiple companies in an industry leverage cooperatively should raise suspicions on the part of oversight agencies. Airline Costs-Airlines have four major components that account for the majority of their costs structure. These costs are aircraft, fuel, labor and ticket distribution. Examining airline annual reports overtime indicate an interesting consistency of these cost factors across the industry.

If airline executives decide to cut costs, a logical starting point would be the top four costs within the airlines. The executives must decide if they can cut aircraft, fuel, labor and distribution? The answer to cutting aircraft is NO because aircraft hold the seats that are sold in order to generate revenue. Cutting aircraft, especially on a hub and spoke system, is a formula for decreasing revenues, not cost savings. Fuel costs are not controlled by the airlines, except in their ability to hedge on fuel prices, but this to be only a temporally limited option-if successful. Labor costs are high in airlines, mostly due to the nature of the work and the unionized work force.

The majority of the labor costs are for pilots and flight attendants, each governed by a different union organization. Negotiating contracts with pilot and flight attendant unions can cause pre-mature graying, thus this option is not a popular one when looking for costs savings at an airline. With advance in telecommunication technologies, executives found a means to decrease ticket distribution costs. This was a logical response by airlines to leverage the information technologies they are so dependent upon.

From Res to Web Ticketing-Airlines have used a variety of ticket distribution channels throughout their existence. From the onset, airlines sold tickets at the airports they served.

Later the ticket counters evolved into back-room reservation centers with banks of phones. A sea change occurred after deregulation. As airlines scrambled to build their hub and spoke networks along the regulated city market pairs they served, they needed many more aircraft and thus many more passengers. Because of their larger geographical focus, each new hub airline needed to feed as many passengers as possible through its hubs via its spokes, and not lose customers to the competition. Airline reservation centers at the time were not of sufficient size or capability to serve the rapidly expanding needs of the airlines. The airlines sought out the travel agents as ticket distribution force because

1. they existed and could immediately be brought into service

2.   they were in most communities the airlines served

3.   the travel agencies would absorb the initial start-up costs saving the airlines money they were spending at airports and on new aircraft

Basically, the airlines chose to outsource ticket distribution after deregulation. Since each airline was in the processes of developing their hubs and trying to draw customers and earn bran loyalty, airlines quickly bid up the commission rates to travel agents.

To increase both the efficiencies of the airlines in terms of yield management and the travel agents in terms of tickets sold per agent, the airlines independently created CRSs replacing the huge paper volumes of flight schedules. These systems also locked travel agents into contracts with airlines, indirectly through the CRSs and the Airline Reporting Corporation (ARC).

Though outsourced, airlines now had some indirect control over their ticket distribution system by owning the technology that the agents depended upon. Airlines began to cut commission rates in 1994/95. If one airline cut commission rates, others followed. This created an environment where each would have a statically equal chance of not losing a travel agent and their customers. Therefore, each airline saved money, and none lost passengers to the other, a solid win for the airlines. In fact, after the first rounds of commission cuts, tickets sold by travel agents actually increased due to the economy and the need for travel agencies to make up the difference in commission rates.

The mid 1990s also brought the Web as a realistic opportunity for airlines to regain total control over their ticket sales and distribution mechanism. Web ticket was found to the be the most cost efficient means of selling tickets, and with cost savings from the already established e-ticket distribution system which require no paper to be printed, mailed, collected, and sorted, cost saving, the Web became an ideal selling platform. While the cost of a travel agent or reservation center was about equal for ticket distribution, Web ticket distribution could cost as little as $2 a ticket.

When multiplying the millions of ticket sold each year, this form of ticket distribution offered substantial savings. Thus airlines, through various carrots and sticks, started to attract customers to their web sites and away from their own reservation centers and travel agents. Carrots included extra frequent flier miles, lower ticket costs and faster service.

Sticks included, lower commission rates for travel agents, surcharge for tickets not sold on an airline's web site, and not having access to the lowest fares available. The movement away from travel agents and airline owned reservation centers continues. Encouraging customers to go to their Web site and purchase tickets is a logical response by airlines to a new technology that allows them to save substantial money on and begin to control the means of ticket sales and distribution.

Tom Sawyer Effect

A travel agent must meet expenses, as do reservation centers, and the majority of the costs to operate these sites are in recurring labor costs. When a ticket is purchased through a Web site, the seller saves the labor cost because most labor costs is shifted directly to the consumer. It is the consumer who purchases the computer, software, and an ISP connection. It is also the consumer who searches the multiple web sites for the "best deal", enters their seat assignment, credit card number, and prints out their e-ticket confirmation on their printer. A large percentage of the labor costs built into cost of distributing an airline ticket is now outsourced directly to the consumer, thus enabling a $1-$2 transaction cost for airline is tickets via the Web. The saving to airlines, and the costs to consumers collectively, are staggering. Assume it takes a person 30 minutes to find, reserve, and pay for a ticket online, and the average per hour wage is $8 per hour. Multiply $8 an hour times the millions of tickets sold over the Web and it is easy to see why an airline, and other industries, would actively seek out this distribution channel.

Smart companies with good marketing have sold the Web to consumers as a fast, efficient, and fun way to purchases goods and services, just as the character Tom Sawyer convinced his peers to whitewash the fence through skillful marketing, manipulation and psychology. However, is the utilization of The Tom Sawyer Effect for ticket sales and distribution in the consumer's best interests long term? Web distribution and the Tom Sawyer Effect we consider to be a positive development in leveraging a technology. However, it is only positive because it enables one more distribution channel. If airlines were to attract all customers to Web sites with lower fares, then remove all other distribution channel, they could/would raise fares with monopoly control over a single distribution channel. This scenario would be very negative for the consumer because the time they would spend on the Web seeking savings would become an embedded requirement without lower fares, not just one of many options as it is today.

MISTAKES OF TRAVEL AGENTS

Travel agents collectively have made some strategic errors over the past 30-40 years that have, in part, led to the circumstances they find themselves in today. The first error was not to develop what came to be known as the CRS. Travel agents were on the verge of initiating such a project, but were convinced that airlines could provide a superior product, faster and more economical, than the travel agent industry. Though this was probably true, the travel agent industry lost a strategic advantage, controlling airline ticket inventory and distribution, when they deferred to the airlines. A second error occurred after the airlines began to develop a joint CRS then eventually individual CRSs. At the initial stage of development, the travel agent industry was offered partial ownership of this technology, which they rejected.

Ownership would have provided travel agent input in the creation of the technology, a share of the profits from the developed technology, and would have slowed or prevented the airlines use of the CRS as a controlling mechanism over the agents. The third strategic error is the belief many agents had, and still have, that they were equal partners with the airlines. What many agents failed to understand is that

1) the airlines controlled many agencies in terms of revenue stream and

2) that partnerships exist only when a mutual benefit exists.

The airlines, through high commissions and overrides, enabled many agencies to exist and prosper. Once the mutual advantage disappeared, airlines mixed commission cuts and Web distribution quickly disassociating themselves with their traditional ticket distribution force.

ORBITZ

Orbitz has been characterized in many different manners in the testimony before this commission. In reality, Orbitz's purpose is multifaceted and should not be construed as being only one thing or another. At minimum, Orbitz is

1. A late attempt at the large airlines to take advantage of the previously active IPO market.

2. A less expensive means to distribute airline tickets on the Web.

3.   A means of consumer data collection for yield management when the airlines continue to sell off their positions in GDSs.

4.   A means of collecting data on other airlines fare/frequencies/schedules, which direct airline Web fares do not allow.

5.   A more efficient means of producing premium pricing for airline tickets of the airline owners.

6.   Competition for Travelocity.com and Expedia.com.

7.   One more venue for airlines to distribute their tickets in order to access as many different population segments possible.

8.   A means of airline-owners taking control/ownership of their ticket distribution channels.

Orbitz serves all of these functions and probably more. Orbitz has lost large sums of money over the past several quarters and the five large airline-owners have chosen to keep Orbitz afloat and not pull the plug. This means that Orbitz is seen as having value, especially long-term. This may be in the form of an IPO, but given the market conditions, it is an iffy bet. More likely though Orbitz as a data collection and distribution mechanism for the airlines is worth more than the sum of the ticket revenue costs which show up on Orbitz's balance sheet. In fact, critical questions are what is the direct and indirect value of

1.   challenging the dominance online of Travelocity.com and Expedia.com for airlines? More competition, which is good for the consumer.

2.   having a less expensive GDS for distribution for airlines? Good for consumers, only if there are multiple GDS options in the marketplace. If Orbitz owner airlines choose to separate themselves from the traditional GDS such as Sabre and Worldspan and

push/pull all distribution to Orbitz, this would be very detrimental to the consumer due to the restricted competition.

3. a tool that allows each of the five airline owners to share data on pricing to maximize yield management? Airlines have used the GDS technology for this type of price signaling in the past, and with a more powerful and flexible platform in Orbitz, one can expect airlines to continue to use this practice since it enables their philosophy of premium pricing.

Because of the absolute reliance of hub airlines on information and information technologies to keep its premium pricing philosophy in place, the true cost savings of Orbitz cannot be found within just the Orbitz LLC but within each of the airline-owners cost sheets.

> ...the greater their [technology owner's] penetration, the greater their competitive advantage. In many contexts this has resulted in room for only one standard worldwide...Whoever owns that standard, even if only in the most indirect of ways, has the opportunity to extract enormous value. This creates a strong incentive to invest in creating such as standard, to ally with others to increase the chance of acceptance, and if necessary, to give away 99 percent of its propriety content to capitalize on the sliver of advantage that remains.

This is a quote from the book Blown to Bits: How the New Economics of Information Transforms Strategy. Interestingly, the authors of this book are with the Boston Consulting Group, the same group hired by the airlines to create Orbitz suggesting that Orbitz, at conception, had this philosophy embedded within its organization. This means that the Orbitz technology and abilities reflect the desire of the owner-airlines to set one standard in the industry and to extract "enormous value."

IDEAS AND REALITIES

The ideal world for any company, including an airline, is to have monopoly control over a market where the maximum price can be charged for an airline seat and all seats are full. Any airline acting in their own and their shareholder's best interest will do everything legal to strategically move their company toward maximum market share possible.

The ideal world for a consumer is to have many companies in the same business all competing for the customer's dollars. Each company will lower its prices, use as many distribution channels possible, and increase service to attract customers. As the companies compete, prices are driven down and service is driven up, allowing the consumer several good choices for any particular product. As you will notice, the ideal worlds of the airline and the consumer are often antithetical. This means that hub airlines are, quite correctly in the business sense, moving towards monopoly or oligopoly control.

Consumers are on the other end of the spectrum where they gain the greatest value from multiple players on a level playing field, both in airlines and airline ticket distribution choices. It is exactly in this canyon separating these two extremes where the role of a government oversight agency should exercise its power and influence to ensure that the market reflects the most options for the consumer.

Most of the large hub and spoke airlines control specific geographical territory as a holdover from the era during regulation and city-pair service. For example, Northwest Airlines has a dominant presence in Memphis, Tennessee, Detroit, Michigan and Minneapolis, Minnesota while other airlines have their major hubs. Because one airline controls a sizeable portion of the flights in and out of these large hub cities, these airports are often described as fortress hubs.

To compete against a fortress hub airline is very difficult for many reasons. One, the fortress hub airline controls many of the "best" landing and take-off slots as well as gate space. Two, records show that when a airline tries to compete with a fortress hub airline on price on a set of city pairs, the hub airline will lower their price to or below the new airline's price to the same destination and often triple or quadruple the number of flights to the same destination. Short term, this is considered competition. Long term, the deep pockets of the hub airline allow it to outlast the new competition, even at a loss on flights, until the new airline pulls service or goes out of business.

At which time the hub airline raises prices again and decreases flight frequency on the city pair route. The dominant airline is able to starve out the new competition due to its overwhelming presence. Most major hubs carriers chose not to compete head to head at each other's hubs. The reasons are rationale. A new airline would enter the market with lower fares and more flights; the dominant hub airline would lower prices and increase flight frequency on the same city pairs as the new competition. In the end, each airline would lose much money on these flights; all the while the consumer is enjoying the inexpensive tickets and high flight frequency. Because of the lose-lose business scenario many "discount" airlines that have tried, and often failed, to enter hub markets.

When hub airlines chose to compete head to head, one airline will lower many of its fares, and especially in those markets where more than one airline serves, often called "price wars". All hub airlines matched the lowered ticket prices in order to avoid loosing customers to the competition. When the hub airlines follow suit, customers enjoy inexpensive air travel and airlines go deep into the red. For the airlines, "price wars" become a zero-sum game in terms of gaining passengers from other airlines since every airline prices the routes almost identically, so statistically every airline would keep, loose and gain the same number of passengers. Pricing wars once again reaffirmed to the airlines that staying within their hubs and using premium pricing is the best business model for success.

If you are consumer in a fortress hub airline city, your airline choices are few and the prices you pay are higher than on routes with more competition, especially for the last minute business traveler. This is due to the lack of competition at that airport on specific city pairs. At present, the best possible scenario for consumers is Southwest Airlines and similar discount carriers. Southwest, with its business philosophy of discount pricing, can enter a market and drive down overall prices on specific routes by offering lower fares. Local hub airlines have to lower their prices to match Southwest's fares and frequency and hope that their frequent flier mileage programs and marketing keep customers loyal.

Southwest has been successful at creating sustained competition at major cities. Likewise, because Southwest is an established airline with deep pockets, fortress hub airlines cannot use the same tactic of starving out the airline as they do with smaller and newer start-up discount carriers. In fact, since Southwest makes a profit on its discounted flights, an airline trying to starve out Southwest would only starve itself. For the consumer Southwest Airlines and similar carriers are the key to inexpensive, safe and good service.

For hub airlines, Southwest is the major threat to their safe and profitable hub networks. The positive benefits for consumers when a discount carrier like Southwest enters and sustains themselves in a market are clear. In this model when of multiple airlines serving the same city pairs, best serves the consumer both short and long term.

This forces airlines to compete head-to-head with lower fares, better service and pushing the technology and customer service envelope in terms of in operational improvements.

POSITIONING

For the foreseeable future, the major hub airlines will continue along the long road of deregulation toward consolidation. The author believes that the US will end up with three major hub airlines, however, which three is hard to guess. As the automobile industry in the 1970s and early 1980s demonstrated so nicely, three or four big companies dominating a market without competition leads to low levels of competition, if any, a low quality product, and a level of arrogance on the part of the companies, all bad for consumers. Decisions post-September 11, 2001, by airline executives will set the stage for which hub airlines will succeed and which will be absorbed by other carriers. Besides the big three, it is expected that Southwest Airlines will continue its steady pace of expansion. Older discount carriers and newer entries such as Jet Blue are also a variable in the equation, but it is difficult at this time to determine their influence and/or longevity.

Airlines will continue to consolidate their control over their ticket sales and distribution. This means that airlines will attempt to route more customers to the Web and away from more costly options. Likewise, from the testimony to date, it appears that the airlines are signaling to each other and the industry that they have a collective strategic plan to move away from traditional GDSs and toward the Web and Orbitz- and most importantly Orbitz as a new GDS- as the primary data collection mechanism for airlines. Routing through Web sites and Orbitz is ideal for the hub carriers because

1. The airline's Web sites offer the least expensive method of ticket distribution since the Tom Sawyer Effect. is in place.

2. Orbitz is owned by member airlines, so any revenue generated through Orbitz is revenue generated for them, though indirectly.

3. If a travel agent in a hub city make a reservation for any hub airline using a new Orbitz GDS, all hub carriers will benefit from every other hub carrier since each will earn a part of the revenue via Orbitz, potentially reducing the need for not only travel agent commissions but also overrides since overrides are based on the desire of airlines for travel agents to route traffic to their airline. If each uses the same Orbitz GDS, then no matter the airline, each airline will gain a portion of revenue through revenue generated through a single conduit. In short, through a revenue sharing arrangement, airline owners could continue ticket sales and revenue generation through their Orbitz, but could remove travel agent overrides without fear of travel agents shifting business to another airline. This would effectively kill more travel agents, much of the traditional GDS revenues and leave one strong player, an Orbitz GDS. Once again, fewer options for the consumer leads to poor service, low quality, high prices and lack of innovation, all of which are negative in a capitalist oriented economic system.

4. An Orbitz GDS would allow a type of insurance policy for airlines in ticket sales and distribution where all costs and revenues are spread across all owner airlines.

5. By evolving Orbitz into the airline preferred GDS, online competition such as Travelocity.com and Expedia.com could be required to pay to access the

Orbitz GDS, increasing the movement of consumers to Orbitz directly and away from the higher costs associated with Travelocity and Expedia due to their potential Orbitz GDS access costs. Removing Travelocity and Expedia from the scene would lead to only one major online travel distribution portal, and that distribution system owned by airlines. Forcing all consumers to one location on the Web for airline ticket distribution is a recipe for monopoly control and higher prices, decreased competition, decreased innovation, and a decline of the dynamic technology-leading US economy since monopoly control reduces the need for innovation.

6. Orbitz, because of its single connectedness with all member airlines, allows a fast and efficient means of indirect communication. If one airline debates raising fares, placing the information in Orbitz would trigger the other airlines to respond in one of two ways. One, match the rate hike, and all respond in kind. Two, do not match the rate hike, and the initial airline removes its rate increases. This practice through Orbitz and the initial launching of the direct-connect technology will make the practice of price signaling seamless. In short, owner-airlines will be able to directly and indirectly via the technology letting each other know what they are doing to maximize their premium pricing plans. Likewise, with all fares flowing through a central node, Orbitz becomes a virtual corporation of the owner-airlines, enabling a virtual merger of the big hub airlines, without the legal restrictions imposed by a direct merger consisting of asset sharing. This scenario is very problematic for not only the consumer, but also the US economy as a whole, which is driven in part by technological innovation. By allowing previously competing entities to collaborate leads to the strong temptation of collusion which

airlines with a premium pricing philosophy will leverage to maximize profitability. With a virtual merger through Orbitz, airlines WILL NOT push the technology envelope in order to serve more customers, improve service, improve quality, and lower prices. This negative environment will lead to a stagnation in a part of the US airline industry. The potential density of this new virtual mega airline to challenge discount carriers like Southwest-the only strong discount bulwark in existence-is also problematic.

For travel agents, this is a brave new world. Travel agencies whose sole source of revenue has historically been airline ticket commissions and overrides must adapt to the new environment or go out of business. Agents and agencies that market themselves for their expert travel services and/or complete business services, will fill a needed niche and continue to grow and produce profits. Travel agents who have shifted their revenue stream from one business (airlines) to another (car rentals, cruises and hotels) are playing Russian roulette because the same economic forces and technologies which enabled airlines to cut commissions and draw passengers toward their own Web sites will be leveraged by the car rental companies, the cruise lines, and hotel chains. To succeed, travel agents must market themselves to the consumer directly, offering a valueadded service that customers are willing to pay a premium to obtain. If travel agents could collectively market themselves to the customer as the premier gatekeepers, then the agencies could obtain more power over various travel and tourism companies vis-à-vis their position to the consumer.

The ideal world for the consumer is competition, both in airlines and in ticket distribution in the market. At present, Southwest Airlines is the most aggressive and competitive airline. Likewise, one cannot intellectually de-link information technologies, hubs and the airlines.

Therefore, as hub airlines are quickly dissolving their relationship with travel agencies and adopt the Web and Orbitz as preferred platforms, red lights should go off and people should ask, why would major hub airlines, who ideally should be rigorously competing, coming together in a distribution network? Why are airlines, which created and owned controlling interests in most GDS now complaining about high GDS prices? The logical scenario emerging is an attempt at a legal consolidation of these large hub carriers. The time is now to address this issue by the oversight agencies

ONLINE BUSINESS TRAVEL MANAGEMENT (BTM)

Nowadays, the business travel has become the second largest corporate cost and corporate travel managers are increasingly being pushed to better control and reduce business travel expenses. Companies are developing stricter and specific processes and policies, but the use of online business travel management (BTM) solutions has appeared to be an effective way to achieve this. Thus, although companies with high travel expenditures traditionally used specialised businesscorporate travel agencies, nowadays they are immigrating to online BTM solutions that are developed either by traditional travel agents that want to reintermediate their business model or by independent software companies that want to enter the lucrative business travel market.

Online BTM solutions aim to streamline and enhance the monitoring of the travel procurement processes of their clients in order to ultimately decrease the latter's travel expenditures while enhancing the provision of travel services. However, online BTM solutions are dramatically changing the dynamics within the tourism distribution chain as well as the inter-relations amongst travel distribution players such as principals (hotels, airlines etc), intermediaries and business travellers' companies.

Although the benefits and impacts of Internet fostered 'e-transformation', 'dis-intermediation' and 'reinter-mediation' have been widely discussed within the generic literature as well as the B2C tourism literature, their impact in the B2B interfirm relations in the tourism distribution chain have received little attention. Moreover, although practitioners are realising the impact of Internet use on building profitable long-term relationships with trading partners, this topic has also received little consideration. On the other hand, a high quality B2B relationship is particularly valuable in the business travel service sector, because credibility of BTM providers and previous experience with them are core parts of the intangible nature of their services. Indeed, customers' perceptions of service quality are often commensurate with their perceptions of the relationship with the service provider.

Impact of Internet on BTM

Internet advances and the proliferation of their travel applications had a dramatic impact on BTM. On the one hand, in their attempt to disintermediate traditional players in the travel distribution chain as well as drive and develop direct relations with their customers on their websites, principals (airlines scheduled, charter or low cost, hotels, car rental companies, train operators etc) are changing their policies mainly in the reduction and recently on the elimination of commissions paid to travel agents. As a result, BTM agencies have to change their business model and pricing strategies by charging their customers fees for their services and working on behalf of them as negotiators for best possible deals rather than being a distributor of the principal.

Moreover, instead of focusing only on big corporate clients, BTM agencies are also increasingly getting interested in the small and medium enterprise market segment by launching dedicated services such as that of Amadeus/e-Travel. Lastly, several BTM agencies have been also adopting information and communication technologies for streamlining their processes and adopting more flexible structures. On the other hand, Internet developments fostered the mushrooming of travel cyberintermediaries and of their business models, as well as enabled an increased online transparency amongst principals' products and their prices.

Consequently, the bargaining power of business travellers has substantially increased, new cyberintermediaries such as Expedia Corporate Travel have entered in the BTM market, while traditional BTM agencies have developed a 'click and mortar' presence in order to survive or reintermediate their business model. In general, the biggest challenge for BTM agencies nowadays is the emergence of business travel e-procurement solutions and online self-booking business travel systems that are primarily developed and used either by independent software companies or GDS or even outsourced to BTM agencies for developing their technological platform. In other words, online BTM solutions have furthered blurred the inter-firm relations and dynamics within the travel distribution chain. These internet based BTM solutions enable companies to take advantage of special business fares and at the same time, they provide controls to track savings, enforce, monitor the obedience and prevent abuses of the travel policies.

Overall, as Internet developments have increased competition and volatility within the BTM market, the way that online BTM solutions are changing and affecting the BTM-businesses relations has not been examined yet. However, research in this area is crucially important nowadays since it can provide very useful practical information and insights on how BTM agencies can exploit eprocurement BTM systems for enhancing and personalising their travel services, increasing the loyalty of their corporate clients and so, locking them in. Thus, the examination of inter-firm relations amongst online BTM agencies and their corporate clients as a result of web-based BTM solutions is the aim of this research whose model and findings are developed as follows.

More recent researches are focusing on investigating the impact of the Internet on the market structure, business models and buyer-seller relations. Preliminary findings suggest that the Internet's impact may differ from industry to industry and from business to business. In this vein, limited research into the internet's impact on B2B relations exists, while further research into the specific impact of online BTM solutions in the BTM-businesses relations is granted. To achieve that, a first step is to review the divergent views found in the literature regarding the impact of the internet on buyers-sellers relations.

Internet-based technologies provide effective and efficient ways of conducting business. On the one hand, buyers can easily and rapidly: gather, analyse and compare information about available suppliers and their products and services; effectively negotiate with suppliers procurement terms and prices; efficiently transfer and place their order fulfilments; and access after-sales services 24 hours. On the other hand, by conducting business electronically, sellers can efficiently gather and effectively data mine and analyse customers' information about marketing, sales and services activities with the aim to develop more direct, personalised and long-term relations with their customers.

However, the pace of change in the e-commerce arena has been so rapid, making it difficult for firms to examine the advantages and disadvantages of different ways of managing interfirm relationships in the dynamic environment of B2B e-commerce. The importance of managing inter-firms relationships emerged when many businesses learnt that they must collaborate with partner firms or even competitors (giving rise to co-opetition models) in order to compete against others. Theories that have been used in order to explain inter-firm relations either online or offline include the transaction costs economics theory, the social exchange theory, the interorganisation theory and industrial network theory . In general, research on buyer-seller relations has mainly been addressed from two perspectives:economic and socio-psychological.

Elements that have been found to affect the development of inter-firm processes and exchange of inter-firm relations have been generally categorised as technical/ structural and social bonds or process and relation integration. To synthesize the literature, the terms of 'social' and 'structural' bonds are also used in this study to categorise the most heavily used elements in the literature. Social bonds are defined as investments of time and energy that produce positive interpersonal relationships and collaborative practices between the partners, although these can range from formal, organisational contacts through to informal, personal ones.

In contrast, structural bonds are forged when two organisations adapt to each other in some economic or technical ways such as product or process adjustments, for example, investments in assets dedicated to their relationship such as e-procurement systems. Specifically, process integration has been defined as the extent to which the various stages in the business process are integrated and information on current processes is being exchanged.

The general consensus in transaction cost economics is that three contextual factors can affect the type (structural or social/relational), dependence and dynamics between inter-firm relations. First factors of asset specificity and availability of alternatives resources: the higher the asset specificity and the fewer the alternative resources the higher the dependency of a firm on its partner. Asset specificity can be defined as structural, specific and high investments (e.g. IT investments or process changes) that are not redeployable outside the relation. However, the Internet and web-based BTM partners use the same open set communication protocols, software and standardised information communication structures.

Overall, as online BTM solutions entail minimal expenditures (i.e. low asset specificity) and high partner flexibility in terms of 'plug and playing' with another online BTM agency (i.e. numerous alternatives), the Internet had a positive impact on developing more 'equal' BTMbusinesses relations. However, the time, cost and change management cost for using online BTM systems are a structural bond. The deployment of online tools requires a lot of preparation from the client perspective (clear travel policies, standard booking procedures, information workflow mapping, job redesign and culture change) and this use to put off several companies in adapting such systems. Generally, one could claim that BTM agencies try to lock-in their clients through 'hidden' online BTM systems' costs, such as training and familiarisation on their software and interface, customisation of their solution to company's needs and collection and analysis of transaction data in order to better learn and meet their customers' needs.

Uncertainty 'the difficulty of making accurate predictions about the future' can also impact on the formation of social and structural elements that may bond and impact interdependence between firms. Uncertainty relates both to the environment and to the behaviour of the exchange partner The first dimension, relates to how difficult it is to predict market conditions, mainly because of increased online market and price transparency as well as because of the diffused difficulty in foreseeing the emergence, future, stability and impact of online BTM solutions. However, quite interesting market conditions and uncertainty did not influence companies' propensity to use online BTM solutions.

On the other hand, the fact that the market of online BTM solutions is still new and emerging without a clear market standard and leader makes corporate clients sceptical on their decision to commit early on one platform. Moreover, the ongoing distrust of online BTM users in the transfer of crucial organisational data through the internet and in data sharing with a third party also act as inhibitor in BTM diffusion and use. The difficulty in estimating the behaviour of the exchange partner is defined as relational uncertainty (or opportunism in the transaction cost theory) and highlights the need of BTM agencies to develop and foster strong relational bonds (such as trust, satisfaction, commitment and good communication tools) in order to develop, maintain and foster long-term collaborative relationships with their corporate clients).

Social bonds are not necessarily independent of structural bonds, that open technological systems and applications can significantly impact the significance and impact of the interplay between social and structural bonds and so ultimately the inter-firm relations and dynamics. So, depending on the situation and context, social bonds may be used for reinforcing, supporting and/or inhibiting structural bonds and vice versa. For example, firms having low levels of process integration are less likely to pose emphasis on relational integration, as well as when operational processes are not shared firms have little to discuss and develop social bonds.

On the other hand, when operational and structural integration is high, the structure and degree of common decision-making and communication processes and so of relational integration can be high and have a greater impact on the outcomes of the relations. In this vein, a firms' dependence on another can be centred on the presence of switching costs that 'lock in' it into the relationship. These switching costs can be created by investments in the form of structural bonds and derived from how satisfied an exchange partner is with the other's performance. More generally, social bonds may need to be in place before knowledge-based structural bonds develop while contractual arrangements between parties in a relationship can be an antecedent to trust. In general, however, opportunities for structural bonding emerge as a result of social bonds being in place.

Developing the Theoretical Model

B2B internet use may facilitate the generation and exploitation of new business opportunities as well as enhance and/or transform inter-firm relationships, resulting in more efficient business and processes. Overall, most literature is conceptual and positive about the internet's potential for facilitating relationships. On the other hand, the limited empirical studies are divided about the potential of internet-facilitated B2B relationships. An empirical study found effective communication, trust, mutual understanding, share of benefits/risks and commitment being important components in relationships between ASPs and their corporate clients.

However, another study in the adoption of e-tourism found that consumers' lack of control over their own personal information and how it will be used is a disincentive to trust businesses and to engage in B2C relational exchanges. Indeed, establishing a relationship with exchange partners may be harder to achieve in an internet environment because alienation reduces the personal social interaction that occurs between individuals in a marketing relationship. When firms begin to adopt the internet in their operations, the attempt to coordinate business activities may be accompanied with distrust, ambivalence and open resistance by exchange partners. However, most of what is known about the potential for internet-facilitated relationships seems to be anecdotal, experiential, ad hoc and descriptive. Moreover, there has been no empirical attempt to test such relationship-facilitating aspects of internet use in a B2B context.

A recent reserach proposes a comprehensive theoretical model (Figure 1), that summarises the relationship-facilitating aspects of web-based BTM solutions in a B2B context. Specifically, the extant literature has speculated on five separate relational bonds without distinguishing them as structural and social bonds, but no empirical evidence exists about how the internet influences them. As shown in Figure 1, social bonds include trust and satisfaction and structural bonds include communication and dependence. Constructs were included in the proposed model only when empirical evidence of their impact on inter-firm relationships was found. The dominant relationships between these constructs that have been studied in a non-internet environment form the basis of this model.

Analytically, the importance of communication for holding a relationship together has been stressed in the literature as the glue that holds together a channel of distribution. Communication and the exchange of information is also characterised as the lifeblood of collaborative inter-firm relations. According to the social exchange literature, effective communication between partners is essential to achieve the intended objectives, as it leads to better informed parties, which in turn should make each party more confident in the relationship and more willing to keep it alive. In turn, dependence is created by partners' relationship investments, that is, asset reciprocity that holds the relationship partners together and creates barriers to leave the relationship because of the high costs involved.

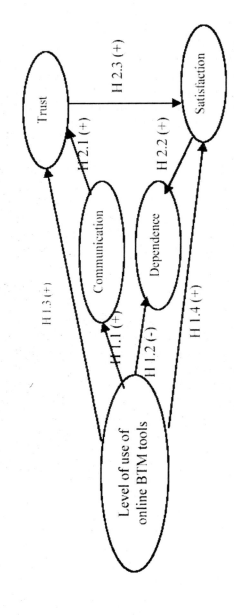

Figure 1. Theoretical model and hypotheses for the impact of online BTM tools on BTM agencies- businesses

The greater the interdependency, the stronger is the relational behaviour. Dependency between organizations results from a relationship in which participants perceive mutual benefits from interactions. Mutual dependency between participants increases when the size of the exchange and importance of exchange are high, when participants consider their partner the best alternative, and when there are few alternatives or potential sources of exchange.

Trust, one of the most frequently quoted social bonds, is viewed as an essential ingredient for successful relationships and concerns exchange partners' confidence and reliability. Trust, an inter-firm relationship quality feature, is conceptualised as 'the firm's belief that the other company will perform actions that will result in positive outcomes for the firm, and it will not take unexpected actions that would result in negative outcomes for the firm".

Trust emerges when partners share a variety of experiences and increased their joint action and participation in the relation, understand one another's objectives and goals and when there is an increased commitment and so reduced uncertainty regarding another's behaviour. Hence, the inputs that generate trust are regular interaction, communication, cooperation, joint actions and decision making, and closeness between the parties to a relationship.

Satisfaction is another social bond frequently mentioned in the literature. Rather than capturing the transient and encounter-specific evaluations and emotions, applied research tends to measure satisfaction as the buyer's general level of satisfaction based on all experiences and activities with the firm. Thus, satisfaction can be defined as an affective response, which is an end-state as the result of appraisals including disconfirmation and perceived performance. Inter-firm relationships' elements such as trust, communication, commitment, dependence and joint activities have been found as antecedents of the quality of inter-firm relationships and of the overall satisfaction of relationships; partners.

The interactivity, convergence and customisation elements of the internet can not only enhance the interchange of information between partners, but also overcome time, technological platform (PDA, PC, mobile phone etc) or geographic limitations as well as multimedia transmission. It is hypothesised that: H1.1: the level of use of online BTM systems is positively associated with communication. The internet may also empower buyers to find lower price suppliers with less search costs and thus serve as a cost-effective alternative form of information-gathering for businesses, enabling the substitution of the exchange relationship. That is, communication efficiencies through the internet may increase the number of suppliers with which a buyer firm can effectively and efficiently exchange. Thus, emerging internet-based inter-firm networks should reduce supplier power and a firm's dependence on a single supplier or a single buyer may be reduced. Thus, it is hypothesised that: H 1.2: the level of use of online BTM systems is negatively associated with dependence.

Regarding the impact of internet use on exchange partners' trust in each other, the following can be argued. Although the internet environment presents relatively few cues by which trust on partners or on electronic transactions can be assessed, studies and system providers nowadays highlight some practical tools for enabling and providing enhanced secure online transactions. The third hypothesis is formed as follows: H 1.3: the level of use of online BTM systems is positively associated with trust.

The internet has the potential to increase customer satisfaction levels, particularly through customisation and personalisation of the technologically delivered service. However, the reduction of involvement of people in the service process is considered to be detrimental to customer satisfaction because some customers still prefer face-to-face rather than electronic contacts. However, preliminary findings in the online BTM market have shown that online BTM systems' users are satisfied with the Internet use even for the booking of complicated travel itineraries that might have required personal, face-to-face contact amongst business travellers and travel agencies staff. It is hypothesised that: H 1.4: the level of use of online BTM systems is positively associated with satisfaction.

Three further hypothesised relationships derive from empirical studies regarding the interaction of the relational bonds in offline inter-firm relationships. Studies reveal communication as a major precursor of trust. Communication is treated as an antecedent of trust, conflict and business understanding. Communication fosters trust by assisting in the resolution of disputes, by aligning perceptions and expectations and by negotiating joint performance metrics and systems for sharing benefits and risks. In this vein, trust amongst interfirm relations significantly enhances satisfaction with business performance and so, trust is a critical determinant of satisfaction. Finally, when the outcomes obtained from the exchange relationship are satisfying and highly valued, then there is a higher level of dependence between exchange partners.

So, higher levels of dependence are associated with higher levels of satisfaction. The three final hypotheses regarding the interrelations amongst relation bonds are as following: H 2.1: Internet-facilitated communication will be positively associated with trust. H 2.2: Trust is positively associated with satisfaction in an online BTM system. H 2.3: Satisfaction is positively associated with dependence in an online BTM system.

The reserach was aimed at examining the inter-firm relations amongst corporate business and their BTM agencies when using internet based BTM systems. To achieve this goal, the literature was reviewed and a model was proposed. For operationalising the constructs of the model, multi-items scales based on past research were used for all constructs except the one for the level of use of online BTM tools. The scale measuring the level of use of online BTM tools reflected the extent to which the online tools are used for BTM functions.

As there was none scale measuring this construct, the research used in-depth interviews with business travel managers and BTM agencies as well as trade publications for identifying the various internet-supported BTM functions. A seven-point semantic differential format was used for 6 measurement items. The scale had a reasonable level of reliability reflecting the care with which it was constructed. The scale measuring communication reflected the credibility, accuracy, frequency, timeliness and meaningfulness of information exchanges. The scale had a seven-point semantic differential format and the items used were adopted from Anderson and Narus. The scale achieved a high level of reliability. The dependence construct was measured with respondent's perceptions of their need to maintain the relationship with the BTM agency to achieve desired goals.

A seven-point semantic differential format was used for the items adopted by Ganesan. The scale achieved a high level of reliability. The satisfaction scale measured an affective reaction to the outcomes achieved in the relationship. The construct was measured using a seven-point semantic differential format and the items used by Dwyer, Schurr and Oh. The scale achieved a high level of reliability. The trust scale measured the confidence a party has in the honesty and integrity of their partner. The scale had a seven-point format and used the items adopted from

Morgan and Hunt. The purified scale displayed a high level of reliability.

For testing the model data were gathered from the corporate travel managers and travel procurement officers of businesses located in the UK, Greece, and Cyprus. This was a purely convenience sample simply available to the researcher by virtue of its accessibility. Contact and address details were found in the Internet and the business travel trade press. Overall, 550 questionnaires were posted or e-mailed to appropriate people and with a followed-up communication after three weeks 194 questionnaires were received giving a response rate of 35.2%.

Respondents represent a varied sample of businesses using online BTM tools: 23% of companies have been suing online BTM tools for more than 5 years, 48% between 1 - 4 years and 29% for less than a year (average duration of the relationship with online BTM agencies 3.4 years); while a great majority of companies (67%) employed more than 100 employees that they usually travel and need travel arrangements. However, also a substantial number of companies (11%) used the online BTM tools for making the travel arrangements for less than 50 of their employees.

The sample size of 194 cases satisfied the general rule of thumb that suggests that sample sizes as low as 100 are adequate, with 200 or more recommended as safe for structural equation modelling. However, a sample size of 194 cases was not sufficient to support a structural equation model at the level of complete disaggregation of measured variables. Hence, the factor scores were used as single item indicators and a path analysis was performed, applying the maximum likelihood estimates (ML) method. Initially, one-factor congeneric models for each set of items were estimated. Sample covariance matrix were used as input into AMOS program to estimate the proposed and competing models.

The one-factor congeneric models not only provided a first test of item reliability and validity, but also served as a means of data reduction in order to obtain a manageable number of manifest [or composite] variables which can be used in subsequent structural equation models. Standardized residuals were used to identify and later remove problematic indicators. This scale purification led to a second stage of full structural modelling where a structural model with all five constructs and their indicators was estimated. The constructs were represented as correlated first-order factors. The indicators were related only to their posited construct. The chisquare statistic of the model was very small and insignificant, indicating a good fit. The other fit measures were indicative of adequate fit to the sample data. Four out of the seven hypothesised relationships were statistically significant while the remaining three hypothesised relationships were rejected.

Analytically, this reserach revealed that online BTM tools enhance BTM agencies- businesses bonding mainly through the enhanced inter-firm communication that is enabled through the internet (H 1.1). So, although online BTM tools were not found to significantly affect and enhance inter-firm constructs such as trust, satisfaction and dependence, the impact of former on partners' communication was evident. BTM agencies should consider and exploit online tools for enhancing communication with their clients as the most vital and critical element for developing competitive business models, enhancing their value proposition and locking-in their clients. In other words, due to the mediating effect of communication, a BTM agency that can manage to use the internet effectively and efficiently to communicate with its corporate clients, will at the same time enhance trust and satisfaction.

Many BTM agencies are currently developing and / or operating customer contact services in order to enable and support their communications with their customers. BTM agencies should also exploit the ubiquitous nature of the internet in order to provide customer-centric and seamlessly integrated multichannel communications (PDA, PCs, mobile phones, call centres etc) to their customers. Concerning, the content of continuous communication that BTM agencies should provide this could vary from travel products and prices (e.g. updates on latest offers, cancellation of flights and change of itineraries etc) to cost management of travel expenditures (e.g. preparation and dissemination of detailed reports analysed per individual customer regarding travel expenditures) and to communication and tools supporting the flow and streamlining of travel expenditure process (e.g. dissemination of travel expenditure reports for approval, management's alerts when travel policies are violated etc). However, future research is required for identifying and assessing the information needs and their importance to different types of corporate business.

The research has revealed that such an argument is not anymore valid. Instead, internet capabilities should be used for enhancing inter-firm communication which in turn due to its mediating effect can further support and foster the social and relational bonds such as trust, dependence and satisfaction that are required for building and maintaining inter-firm relationships. The exploitation of the Internet capabilities for enhancing inter-firm relationships and the creation of relational and structural bonds between firms is also supported by the 'move to the middle hypotheses', initially argued by Clemons et al. and later found to be supported in different industries.

According to the 'move to the middle hypotheses' information technology applications move firms away from market to intermediate governance structures characterised by increased outsourcing of business functions but from fewer suppliers. In other words, the 'move to the middle hypotheses' provides evidence of the successful exploitation of IT capabilities by outsourcing suppliers in order to reduce uncertainties and risks related to market governance forms and lock-in their partners for longer periods of time. However, findings are limited to only one type of service and to three countries that have specific economic, business and cultural characteristics. The generalisability of the findings are also limited due to the fact that other industries may also differ in terms of the extent of internet adoption, employees skills and attitudes in Internet use and benefits. This is because an industry characterised by greater or lesser internet adoption may exhibit different patterns of communication within it and subsequently, experience a different effect on exchange relationships. Thus, it is evident that future studies should try to enhance, test and further enrich this model by conducting larger scale and cross-industry studies.

9

AVIATION TAXATION

Air transportation is a crucial enabler of global economic activity. It facilitates the movement of business personnel, serves as a key input into fast-growing industries such as tourism, and allows the vital interactions necessary to sustain many modern, high-technology, service industries. It performs a central role in meeting the evolving trading needs of the world, as internationalization and globalization become increasingly important to the nation's economy.

In addition to its economic role, air transportation serves important social functions, not only meeting the access needs of remote, small communities, but also facilitating continuing contact between members of geographically dispersed families-an increasingly common feature of modern society. The nature of air transportation, however, superficially makes it a convenient subject of indirect taxation. As a high-revenue (though not high-profit) sector with relatively few suppliers, aviation tax collection is inexpensive and convenient for the Treasury. And as an industry air transport is politically vulnerable, lacking any large voting block to protect its interests.

There is also an ingrained common perception, largely misplaced in the twenty-first century (after 25 years of economic deregulation and with the widespread availability of the services of low-cost air carriers), that taxation of air transportation constitutes a tax on a luxury good. This is simply not true. Today over 40 percent of airline trips are taken to visit friends and relatives and over 25 percent occur on low-cost carriers.

Nevertheless, over the years a plethora of taxes has been imposed on America's airlines, in addition to the generic corporate taxes levied in the United States. These taxes have risen substantially over time, creating a burden that has not been more broadly shared by industries. By 2000, the airline contribution to U.S. excise tax revenues had already climbed to 14 percent, up from just four percent in 1971. These special aviation taxes are imposing an excess burden on airlines and, ultimately, adversely affect not only the commercial viability of many carriers but also the vitality of the nation's economy and the social welfare of its citizens. This is not to say that the airlines should be exempt from contributing to an efficient taxation regime-rather, it is a matter of equity and structure.

Inappropriate taxes, either in terms of their magnitude or their form, can seriously distort the market for air transportation services. Because the demand for airline products is often derived from the final demands of society for goods and services, as well as from the desire for individuals to travel for leisure purposes or to meet friends and relatives, distortions to ticket prices have the potential of adversely affecting national output and the larger welfare of the country. In particular, they penalize those industries most reliant on high-speed, scheduled transportation-industries generally having the greatest potential to improve and sustain the nation's economic wellbeing.

The development of sound taxation policy must consider administrative features, downstream implications for production and consumption, and effects on various income groups and communities. While aviation taxes, at least on some criteria, do well regarding aspects of the first of these features, in that they are cheap and easy to administer, they fall short in virtually all respects in terms of both downstream efficiency and equity.

Truly efficient taxation minimizes distortion to the relative levels of consumption of different goods and services. Aviation taxation fails this test, wherein multiple forms and rates apply. Further, efficient taxes are levied on final output, rather than on intermediate inputs such as transportation. Taxing an input yields unpredictable outcomes (i.e., "downstream effects") on final consumption and often creates perverse disincentives for the intermediate supplying industries.

Equity considerations entail the imposition of higher taxes on luxury goods and services that are consumed by wealthier people. But air transportation is now remarkably affordable and widely used by all strata of American society. One can also point to the considerable subsidies that Amtrak receives to carry passengers over routes that compete directly with the airlines. Since a large percentage of rail users are middle- and high-income, it seems perverse that Amtrak is heavily subsidized while airlines offering parallel services are being taxed.

Taxes are sometimes used as a form of social engineering to discourage consumption of socially undesirable products such as tobacco or alcohol. Again, however, the tax structure is hardly consistent. Someone paying $75 to an airline for a non-stop round-trip ticket pays an additional $25 in taxes and fees, and someone paying a base fare of $300 for a double-connection flight pays over $50 more. Contrast these rates of 35 percent and 27 percent respectively to the 18 percent federal excise tax on cigarettes and the 11 percent federal excise tax on whiskey.

Some taxes paid by the airline industry are seen as hypothecated user fees rather than general taxation, essentially intended to fund expanded airport capacity and air traffic control services. Airlines should pay for the facilities that they use. However, the taxes and their applications are tenuous in terms of reflecting a genuine charge for services provided by the taxing authority, and there is no mechanism that ensures that the resultant revenues are spent effectively.

A comparison of taxes paid by commercial aviation with those paid by non-commercial aviation, relative to their respective use of the nation's airways, reveals considerable cross-subsidization enjoyed by the latter. Such cross-subsidies are not only highly inefficient but also inequitable, given the respective income levels of commercial and general aviation (GA) users. Analysis of the downstream effects of aviation taxes on particular industries, regions, or groups of individuals is insightful. From a number of case studies it is clear that the current regime of aviation taxation damages the development of industries that make extensive use of air travel, and is having particularly adverse effects on some geographic regions.

In some cases, taxation limits the movement of individuals into markets by heightening the costs of transportation, the tourist industry being the most obvious case. Reducing the tax burden on those wishing to fly to Florida, for instance, would act as a stimulus to local travel-based industries, as well as having expenditure-multiplier implications. Scenario analysis indicates that removing the federal ticket tax could, depending on how travelers choose their services and routings, produce some 77,000 additional jobs in the state. Reducing or eliminating the passenger facility charge (PFC) or federal security surcharge could also yield powerful economic benefits. Removing the former could generate over 35,000 jobs.

Air transportation also serves the function of moving personnel around, and facilitates the more efficient conduct of business. High-tech industries make particularly extensive use of air transportation-its personnel flying about 60 percent more than equivalents in more traditional industries. Examination of high-tech activities in the National Capital Region around Washington, D.C., which have concentrated in the region in part due to good domestic and international airline access, suggests that the removal of the federal ticket tax would yield a sizeable increase in jobs.

There are also wider social costs associated with inappropriate taxation that are less easily quantified. One of these concerns safety. Air transportation has an enviable safety record, and any additional burden on fares or service quality leads to transfers to less safe transportation modes. Applying widely used parameters, the current federal security surcharge may be resulting in up to 100 additional annual road fatalities at a cost between $99 million and $297 million in fatalities alone. The inclusion of injuries and property damage would inflate this toll.

The overall findings herein were well summarized in the conclusions of the Baliles Commission of 1993: "We took very seriously our charge to examine tax policy and the many fees imposed on the industry. Although the Commission concluded that tax changes alone will not restore the industry to profitability, we believe there are several tax provisions that impede the ability of the industry to return to financial health. We believe those provisions violate reasonable principles of common sense and good public policy and we are of the opinion changes must be made to relieve the airline industry's unfair tax burden."As the case studies show, high taxation on air travel produces deleterious social and economic outcomes, namely:

— reducing one or more aviation taxes would yield additional employment in regions especially dependent on aviation, such as tourism-rich Florida;

— the business community is adversely affected by high taxes, especially highly aviation-dependent industries such as high-tech and tourism; and

— for taxation on air travel to surpass materially taxation on other modes of intercity travel-specifically auto and rail-is inequitable and contrary to sound public policy.

Taken in the aggregate, the current aviation tax structure is causing measurable harm to the national economy. A more rational federal aviation tax regime-in scope, scale, and structure-would be far more likely to stimulate growth and employment in key sectors whose fate is closely tied to air services. While this should be of immediate interest to tourism- and high-tech-dependent communities and constituencies, it should also generate additional tax revenue for the General Fund of the Treasury as the growth of "ripple" industries accelerates, thereby benefiting society at large.

The existing taxation of airlines, while often administratively convenient and politically expedient, is not efficient, as it a tax on an intermediate service rather than on final consumption. To fully reap the demonstrable economic benefits of commercial air transportation, airlines must be treated as economic assets rather than as a source of sumptuary taxation. Air travel should not be treated as a luxury good, but as a necessary and normal service consumed by all strata of society. While in the past airline travel may have largely been the prerogative of the wealthy, commercial air travel is now a mode of transportation used by ordinary people and should be taxed accordingly.

When considering the taxation of airlines, full cognizance should be taken of aviation's role in facilitating the nation's external trade. The economy is increasingly part of a global marketplace, and airlines are a major contributor to the nation's global competitive position. But the current regime of aviation taxation hinders the performance of airlines in larger international markets, ultimately hurting the trade balance and eroding overall revenues.

Airlines should pay the economic costs of resources that they consume and from which they directly benefit. The claim, however, that some elements of aviation taxation represent a "user charge" or "user fee" is difficult to substantiate. The taxes do not provide the incentives associated with fees nor do they act as indications of where capacity needs to be varied. Airlines often pay for items that are of no use to them. Airlines should pay directly for the inputs that they use and not pay arbitrary "user fees" that bear no relation to the economic costs involved. Similarly, the burden of taxation is not efficiently distributed between the various types of air transportation infrastructure users. Business aviation, which is used almost exclusively by high-income travelers, makes extensive use of aviation infrastructure and creates considerable congestion within the system. Policymakers should reassess-indeed reallocate-the relative burdens of taxation on commercial aviation and business aviation, as well as public use, to ensure that the latter pays its fair, proportionate share.

Many twenty-first century industries, such as tourism and high-tech activities, rely disproportionately on air transportation. These are often the industries that enjoy high growth and will continue to contribute income and employment to the nation's economy. These industries make considerable use of air transportation and high levels of taxation impede their growth. The taxation of airlines should be designed so as not to stymie the potential of dynamic industries important to national prosperity.

When considering taxation of airlines, due account should be taken of the negative effects of diverting passengers to more dangerous forms of transportation. After their initial imposition in the World War II era, aviation taxes later served to derive revenue from what was then-in the 1950s and 1960s-considered a luxury good. In the early 1970s, policymakers and airlines agreed on a new rationale for aviation taxes-to develop and maintain the nation's airport and airway infrastructure. But subsequent years added a patchwork of expanded taxes and fees, without commensurate expansion of aviation infrastructure.

In the 1980s, 1990s, and early 2000s government agencies levied new charges for everything from general deficit reduction, to homeland security, to environmental protection, to the subsidization of noncommercial airports and operations, along with pertinent inefficiencies in the relevant regulatory agencies. Now that the commercial aviation has entered a new phase of deregulation-indeed a new era of operation in this twenty-first century, it is time for the tax regime to do the same. The rationale for aviation taxation must be rethought and its structure modified accordingly, factoring in its economic relevance and the critical outcomes enumerated herein.

Taxes serve a purpose. The government requires revenue to fulfill its numerous functions, and there is no reason why the air transportation sector should not, in an appropriate way, contribute to the national treasury. The crucial issue for the airlines is thus not taxation per se, but rather its level, structure, and impact. Because it is somewhat concentrated-which makes revenuegathering relatively cheap for the collection agency-and often perceived as a provider of a luxury service, the airline industry is especially vulnerable to high levels of taxation. These factors sub-optimally limit the growth of the air transportation, because ultimately taxes are either passed on in the form of higher fares and cargo rates or reduced levels of service, especially in a highly competitive environment.

In the short term, particularly in today's marketplace for air services, the taxes are not passed on but rather absorbed by the airlines in the form of weakened financial results. Yet even when the airlines bear the immediate burden of taxation, businesses and individuals must adjust downward their levels of service, either in quantity or quality, to be able to absorb the tax. Taxation invariably distorts markets. Therefore, a well-structured tax regime should minimize the distortions that it imposes downstream on the various sectors of the economy. In the context of airlines, these distortions take a number of forms:

— the taxation of airlines is disproportionately high, retards the industry's development vis-à-vis the overall growth in the economy, and limits its potential contribution to economic wellbeing;

— the level of taxation distorts competition with other transport service suppliers (e.g., differential taxation on rail versus air transportation on the northeast corridor routes);

— the structure of taxation imposes burdens further up the air-services value chain, thus imposing additional costs on the airlines and their customers;

— taxation influences the competitive position of domestic airlines versus international competitors in increasingly global air transport markets; and

— taxation disguised as government-imposed user charges results in:

(i) services being supplied to the airlines in excess of the level the airlines would purchase in an open market ("gold plating"),

(ii) those services being supplied inefficiently, or

(iii) the masking of government obligations to serve unrelated public policy objectives (i.e., customs, border protection) under the guise of user "services."

BASIS FOR TAXATION

Taxation is inevitably a contentious issue. No one likes paying taxes. Taxes have led to wars, and are an ongoing issue for most sectors of the economy. But they are important as a means of financing government activities, providing public goods, and as a mechanism for bringing about social transfers to protect the less well-off in society. It is important, therefore, that the forms of taxes imposed serve the public interest rather than being arbitrary or capricious.

In considering the structure of the taxation regime, it is useful to put the aviation taxation system within the more general framework of taxation. One of the main problems encountered in the past when reviewing aviation taxes is that they were seldom assessed as an entity. Rather, marginal changes have been critiqued, or additional taxes commented upon. It is thus within general taxation principles that aviation taxes are initially examined here.

Taxation involves the compulsory transfers of monies from the general public (individuals and companies) to the government.It takes a diversity of forms, but all affect consumption levels, profits, incentives and welfare distribution. Taxation can occur at any point in the circular flow of income (consumption, expenditure, investment, international trade), but where it lies and the form it takes affects the level, speed, and distribution of this flow between companies, households and government.Taxes on income and wealth are direct taxes, whereas those on consumption are indirect taxes.

Aviation taxation is largely an indirect tax paid to the authorities by the provider of airline services, but the incidence of the taxation is borne more widely, as part of the burden is passed on to travelers and shippers. The amount passed on depends on the conditions of supply and demand in the relevant transport markets. During times of intense competition for budget-minded, Internet-empowered customers, such as the present, the economic incidence of the tax shifts principally to the airline, rather than the consumer. When there are few economies of scale on the supply side and the market for a product is highly competitive, the incidence of any tax is largely pushed down to the consumer in the form of fewer services.Any initial attempts by airlines to push up fares tend to be eroded by competitive pressures.

If airlines cannot pass on the full burden, potential users of air services will find the available quantity and variety of services to be reduced, as some carriers leave the market and others adjust operations in light of the higher costs they now incur. This reality limits the welfare of individuals who wish to make trips and the economic vitality of industries that use air travel or air cargo as a significant input to production. Accepting, however, that there may be valid macroeconomic reasons for taxation to provide public goods and, as part of necessary governance, the issue then becomes one of the types of taxes to use, their relative levels, and the nature of their application. The usual criteria for a "good" tax are that it should be administratively simple and cheap, efficient and equitable.

Administrative Simplicity

For some, a successful tax is simply one that raises more revenue than it costs to collect. This naive accountancy argument, however, says nothing about efficiency or equity in the actual collection of the tax. Administrative factors are considered important for several reasons, including the following:

— The assessment, administrative, policing, and collection activities associated with taxation can be costly, and there are problems in ensuring that these transaction costs are minimized. Administrative simplicity can be viewed as minimizing these costs of tax collection.

— There are often correlations between situations where costs of tax collection are low and the difficulties of gaining political acceptance are minimized; this generally occurs when the number of firms that directly pay the tax is small. There are relatively few airlines, compared to software companies, construction, trucking, medical care, or car repair shops; hence, the administrative costs of tax imposition are small. Taxes on aviation services place much of the cost of collection and administration on the airlines, which have no votes in the determination of a tax. It is easy to see why fiscal authorities find airlines an attractive tax base.

— Administrative efficiency and long-term fiscal planning of the economy also entail having a good idea of the amount of revenue any tax will raise, and a continuity of income from taxes. This generally favors stable markets where demand does not fluctuate significantly over time. But recent demand for air transportation has been volatile with regard to systematic business-cycle effects and is regularly subjected to "system shocks" such as September 11, SARS, oil price variations, and the War in Iraq. The airlines themselves have difficulties in cost recovery and there has been a regular flow of bankruptcies in the industry. The pattern of post-deregulation returns shows airline revenues generally rising with time. A more detailed examination, however, shows considerable variations in this growth path even before the tragic events of September 11, 2001. In recent years, revenues have been falling. This poses particular problems from an administrative perspective because it has also been a period when additional taxes have been initiated and existing ones increased.

— There is also the issue of the "golden goose." The short-term revenue situation is not the only important consideration; a sound tax base also should exhibit long-term vitality. The effects of business cycles are especially pronounced, and the low historical returns on capital reveal an industry lacking monopoly profit to extract for redistribution in the broader economy.

Economic Efficiency

Efficiency in taxation policy is concerned with the implications for those who bear the burden of the tax-i.e., the downstream effect. Depending on the form of the taxation, extraction of monies by the state can reduce individual spending, curb corporate investment, distort relative prices, thwart innovation, and adversely affect international trade. Efficiency in taxation is, therefore, about minimizing distortion from the untaxed situation.As with administrative considerations, aviation taxes may pose problems for downstream efficiency:

— The basic notion underlying an excess burden is that raising a given sum of revenue by different forms of taxation, assuming equivalent collection costs, affects the costs to taxpayers in different ways. Ideally, this burden should be minimized. This is more easily done when the tax system is simple, and its various implications on different groups are transparent. One means of minimizing the excess burden of indirect taxation is to follow the "Ramsey Principle," whereby the tax rate is set according to the elasticity of demand for the items being taxed. If the quantity of the product demanded is highly price sensitive (highly elastic), then it should be taxed less than a product for which demand is much less elastic. It is clear from recent changes in consumption patterns and, in particular, the relative amount of income now spent on air travel as fares have fallen, that the demand for air service is, in the aggregate, quite sensitive to price levels.

— Taxation affects the relative prices of services and the competitive position of industries supplying similar types of service-namely automobile and railway transportation in the case of airlines. Taxes associated with car travel have generally not risen post-9/11. Whereas airlines are now responsible for the "September 11fee" and the aviation security infrastructure fee (ASIF), both of which the current administration has attempted to increase more than once, drivers crossing into Canada or Mexico are not subjected to any such fees. Nor are they subjected to international departure or arrival taxes, immigration fees, customs fees, or agricultural inspection fees.

— There are practical problems in raising target amounts of revenue. It is easier to forecast exactly how much will be raised by an indirect tax if demand for the product is inelastic. If the sales of a good or service do not fall much as a tax is imposed, or increased, it is comparatively easy to predict how much revenue will be collected. Because air travelers are price-sensitive and demand is heavily cyclical, the airline industry is not a predictable source of excise tax revenue.

— Airlines provide an intermediate input into a diverse range of other intermediate activities (business travel) and final consumption (leisure travel), and are a major transporter of high-value cargo. If deemed necessary to tax air services as a proxy for taxing final consumption, considerable care must be exercised to minimize distortions in the final marketplace.

Equity

Equity is inevitably subjective. This does not mean, however, that some broad, socially accepted principles are not normally applied when looking at who pays a tax.

— Normally, progressive taxes are favored, with higher-income groups absorbing the greatest burden. While air transportation was once a luxury item, technology changes of the 1960s and 1970s such as wide-bodied planes and jet engines-along with the managerial reforms that followed deregulation (i.e., hub-and-spoke operations; computerized reservation systems, low-cost carriers)-reduced costs and fares considerably. In 2003, over 70 percent of domestic U.S. passengers had access to low-cost carrier service, up from 30 percent a decade ago.

— In recent years, the long-standing link between national income and spending on air travel has fallen from 1.1 percent of gross domestic product (GDP) to 0.7 percent. This pattern is not one consistent with air travel being a luxury good where consumption rises faster than or at the same pace as income, but rather reflects a more generic good that is part of everyday consumption by ordinary people. Indeed, in terms of income groupings, Amtrak clientele tend to be the wealthiest group of public transportation users. The percentage of Amtrak passengers with incomes below $20,000 per year is the lowest of any intercity mode of transportation and the percentage with incomes above $40,000 is the highest.

— Within the broad realm of social equity, there is also a general tendency to favor taxing items that are in some way seen as anti-social (e.g., tobacco, alcohol). In this context, former presidential advisor Lawrence Lindsey raised the following interesting question, "Federal taxes and fees now consume 25 percent of the cost of a low-priced [airline] ticket. That does not include the further tax burden on profits and wages that most businesses face. This tax compares with an 18 percent federal excise tax on cigarettes and an 11 percent federal excise tax on whiskey. Is air travel more a sin than alcohol or tobacco?"If airlines provide a public bad akin to alcohol or tobacco, then such a rate of tax is justified, but few subscribe to this position.

TAXATION AS A USER CHARGE

The links between tax revenues and their expenditure can take a number of different forms. The majority of tax revenues are not earmarked but rather are channeled into the Treasury or General Fund, to be used by various departments and agencies. The underlying idea is that this gives flexibility in the ways resources are used which can be important as part of larger macroeconomic fiscal policy. The system also provides government with the opportunity to transfer resources for efficiency or equity reasons between citizens, industries and regions as part of larger public policy.

User fees are often seen as payments for a government service that is used so widely that payments at the immediate point of consumption are not practical. In other cases, as with gasoline taxes, they are used as a proxy for consumption, because when motorized traffic first appeared direct collection of a road price involved high transactions costs with manual tollbooths. But a genuine user fee directly relates the costs of an activity to the fees that are collected. A critical issue is, therefore, the way in which the taxes are determined for this hypothecation. Such fees, because they are not direct prices, are generally very much a second-best means of paying for a facility.

The existing system of taxing U.S. aviation fails most of the criteria applied to an appropriate user fee, namely:

(i)   influence the user in such a way that the facility is used efficiently,

(ii) provide guidance as to where capacity changes are needed, and

(iii) generate revenue to finance additional capacity.

The revenues collected from general aviation fall far short of attributable costs imposed on the air traffic control system. Taxes on aviation are numerous and diverse, but they do not even approximate the opportunity costs of the resources used by airlines either in magnitude or in the specifics of individual services. The ticket tax and the segment tax were initially designed to pay for capital needs, but have evolved into a source of funding to cover the bulk of the FAA operating budget. The ticket tax is also driven by the state of supply and demand on any route rather than by factors such as distance, time or duration of travel, or phase of operation. The segment tax bears a closer relationship to the number of takeoffs and landings, the more resource-intensive phases of flight.

The system offers no guidance as to where capacity is under pressure, and thus where additional investment is needed. The taxes on aviation do generate revenues but there is no mechanism to ensure they are funneled into appropriate capacity. There is a danger that with the lack of an immediate link between those paying the taxes and those spending them, expenditures have little connection with the tax preferences of the taxpayers.There is, for example, the prospect of "gold plating," with those spending the tax revenues providing facilities in scale and quality that are well beyond those sought by the taxes payers. The problem is that those spending the tax revenues have no commercial incentive to provide low-cost capacity or to minimize cost. Indeed, scale and complexity may be an attraction for them. A recent GAO study of airport security highlights some of the intrinsic problems of ensuring that user-funded expenditures provide value for money.

One argument for aviation taxation is to finance the air traffic control system. Indeed, although there have been attempts at raids in the past, there is a clear mandate for earmarking specific revenues for this purpose.

Federal Aviation Administration (FAA) efforts to modernize the air traffic control system over the years have not, however, been conspicuous by their success. In particular, there is evidence of a lack of ability for spending institutions to learn in the way that institutions more closely tied to markets do.o Treating taxes as user fees poses problems of macroeconomic management. Monies in large hypothecated accounts (such as the Airport and Airway Trust Fund) are often not spent in a manner consistent with commercial criteria. Often expenditures are governed more by macroeconomic policy considerations rather than by the requirements of the particular sector in question.

On other occasions, funds are "raided" and spent elsewhere. Passenger facility charges, unlike the Airport and Airway Trust Fund, can be used to make payments for debt service or indebtedness incurred while carrying out a project, as well as to finance eligible airport-related projects. While a substantial portion of the revenues from these charges goes to making interest payments on bonds, the remainder is essentially a "prospective charge" on existing users to finance future improvements. The system also reflects a fundamental problem with the Airport and Airway Trust Fund; there is no mechanism that ensures costs are minimized.

Because competition is intense on many deregulated international routes, the commercial viability of carriers depends on their relative cost structures and the fares they can levy. Taxation forms part of this cost base. From a wider perspective, high levels of taxation on international transport not only impose a burden on the industries that pay them, but also act as a secondary form of non-tariff barrier, pushing up the costs of trade more generically.While strict comparisons are somewhat data-prohibitive, we do know that air transport is heavily taxed in many countries, impeding international trade and growth.

The number and level of aviation taxes has risen considerably over time, both in absolute terms and relative to other forms of federal excise taxation. The Airport and Airway Trust Fund began with $564 million in 1971, and airline-based taxes composed some 3.3 percent of all excise-tax receipts for that fiscal year. The proportion, except for a brief period in the mid-1980s, increased again to reach a peak in 1999, when it accounted for 14.4 percent of total excise taxes collected. Today, it constitutes over 13 percent of federal excise-tax revenues. Where taxation is deployed primarily for revenue-collecting purposes,policymakers should aim to minimize market distortions from its inevitable price and income effects. Equity considerations become more complex when account is taken of the ways in which the tax revenues are spent. Finally, there are a range of administrative issues centered about the collection and the administration of taxes.

Aviation taxation has clear merit from an administrative perspective - it is relatively easy for the authorities to collect and, because it is collected from a few companies, is largely hidden from voting public. In that sense it is a soft target for fiscal policy. Beyond that simplistic criterion, however, policymakers must consider equity and downstream efficiency. In general terms, there seems no reason to treat aviation taxes as a source of sumptuary taxation revenues. Air travel is now widespread and used by all strata of American society. It is important in the facilitation of social cohesion as families become more geographically dispersed and as globalization brings large numbers of permanent migrants and short-term workers into the country. Additionally, the International Civil Aviation Organization (ICAO) has estimated that somewhere in the order of 30 percent to 40 percent of world trade by value is now moved by air transportation.

Equally, the taxation of intermediate goods and services such as air travel is not in line with sound principles of taxation. The notion that aviation taxes form user charges is to be examined in more detail, but generally the rationale for taxation as a user charge does not seem applicable in the case of airlines.

EFFECTS OF AVIATION TAXATION

Transportation is recognized as a major facilitator of national economic growth, vital for the creation and sustainability of social and political networks. Locally, the availability and quality of transportation affects the growth of regional and urban economies, and transportation regularly emerges as one of the key factors that influence the location of firms. Air transportation plays an important role in modern justin-time logistics, providing a rapid and reliable means of moving cargo, personnel, and documentation that facilitate the supply chain. It also helps maintain fluidity in labor markets, allowing workers, when moving to new locations, to retain contact with their families and friends.

Air transportation has taken on many of the roles formerly served by surface transportation modes, and added new functions and services. As summarized a few years ago by the National Commission to Ensure a Strong Competitive Airline Industry, "The air transportation system has become essential to economic progress for the citizens and businesses of the nation," but it also concluded, "Tax policies often have had a major and adverse effect on the [airline] industry."

One of the most immediate ways of gaining insight into the societal importance of air transport is to consider the benefits of quality air transport services for local economies. The impacts of air transportation are regularly demonstrated in the analysis done to justify the building or expansion of an airport, or when secondary construction is undertaken, for example, to improve road access to an airport. Since it is not the airport itself that provides transport services, the analysis allows assessment of the importance of air services to the local communities. Quantitatively, the economic impact of access to quality air transportation depends largely on the time frame examined and on the geographical space under review.

In broad terms, airports have four potential economic impacts of varying duration and spatial coverage, including:

— *Primary effects.* These are the benefits to a region derived from the construction or expansion of an airport to allow for more air services-the design of the facility, the building of the runways, the construction of the terminals and hangars, and the installation of air traffic navigation systems. These effects represent one-time injections of expenditure into the local economy with associated employment in industries involved in airport planning, construction and development.

— *Secondary effects.* These are local economic benefits of running and operating air services-employment in maintaining the airport and handling the aircraft, cargo, and passengers. These secondary effects can be extremely important to local employment, income, and tax revenue.

— *Tertiary effects.* These stem from the stimulus to a local economy resulting from firms and individuals having air services at their disposal. These differ for those living in hub cities, compared with those on a spoke or having no major carrier. Airline hubs generally offer more direct flights favored by business travelers. But the airline hub can also benefit those residing in spoke cities because a hub-and-spoke structure offers more service to more communities than a competing pointto-point network. Given that over half of the 15,000 U.S. city pairs served by a major carrier have less than one passenger per day, such interconnectivity is critical to domestic transportation flows.

— *Perpetuity effects.* These reflect the fact that new forms of economic growth, once started in a region, becomes self-sustaining and may accelerate. Availability of good air transportation links can change the entire economic structure of a region. Florida's transformation from a principally agriculturebased economy to one with a large and profitable tourist sector is one such example, as are some of the high-tech clusters that emerged. Although this type of dynamic economic impact of air services is the most difficult to quantify, it is among the most important.

AIR TRANSPORTATION AND HIGH-TECH EMPLOYMENT

Air transportation is crucial to many industries in facilitating trade and commerce across geographic areas. The global economy is becoming more service-driven and less reliant on traditional manufacturing, and the migration to a service economy includes the proliferation of high-tech activities. The Armington Index, often used in industrial analysis, categorizes a wide range of geographical mobile industries employing skilled workers by extracting them from the North American Industry Classification System (NAICS). It includes, among others, elements of: electronic equipment including computers; instruments and related products; business, engineering and management services; transportation services; hotels and motels; insurance carriers, agents, brokers and services; legal services, educational services; financial services; repair services; and communications. On this basis, about 90 percent of the jobs are in metropolitan areas, the vast majority of which are concentrated in fewer than 60 metropolitan statistical areas (MSA).

The changing structure of the global economy has brought with it modifications in demands for air transportation services. These newer industries are more footloose, both nationally and internationally, and personnel make greater use of air transportation when conducting business. Some have estimated that high-tech workers fly 60 percent more than comparable employees in the traditional manufacturing, processing, and extractive industries.One reason for this phenomenon is the range of domestic and international markets served by high-tech industries.

Numerous studies suggest that air transportation can act as a catalyst for high-tech-and high-income-employment. Surveys of high-tech companies, reinforced by econometric analyses of geographical patterns of high-tech employment growth, have shown access to high-quality air service to be a major factor in determining where to locate.Hubs, because of the extensive range of destinations they link, seem particularly attractive to this type of business. Indeed, analysis of the United States by Button and others indicates that the presence of an air hub can add as many as 12,000 high-tech jobs to a regional economy.International air services, too, are becoming increasingly important as facilitators of high-tech growth in a global environment. Additional destinations and frequencies have attracted high-tech employment to hub cities.The National Capital Region Employing a narrower definition of the high-tech sector than the Armington Index, the National Capital Region-the D.C., suburban Maryland, and northern Virginia-boasts significant high-tech employment across a range of sectors that rely on air transportation to retain ties with markets and suppliers. The region is one of the largest in terms of U.S. high-tech employment. Additionally the region is a major tourist attraction with about 12 million leisure visitors descending on Washington annually. This sector also relies heavily on air transportation services.

The region's three major airportshave grown considerably in recent years and offer a wide array of destinations served by global network carriers and low-cost domestic operators. Collectively, with 34 million origin-destination (O&D) passengers, the region was the fifth-largest source of domestic air travelers in 2003 among cities with multi-airport capacity. Analysis of Baltimore-Washington International Airport's catchment area indicates that airline access generated some $6.5 billion for the Maryland economy in 2000, much of it in high-tech-related activities. The total number of jobs directly or indirectly supported by air transport in the area was estimated at 97,000. Analysis of Washington Dulles and Reagan National, using a slightly different criterion, indicates that air services contributed about $9.5 billion in revenue and 162,000 jobs for the airports' catchment areas in 2002.

TOURISM AND AIR TRANSPORT

As incomes rise, the demographics of population change, and work practices evolve, so leisure activities become more important. As a result, the global economy enjoys a robust tourism industry. In 2001, the United States received over 121 million visitors, the vast majority coming by air. U.S. Department of Commerce data show that 4.3-5.3 million people were employed in the U.S. tourist industry in 1997, up from 3.7-4.4 million in 1992. This sector accounted for 4.7-5.6 percent of GDP and had been growing annually at 6.6 percent since 1992. The National Parks, for example, generate about $10 billion a year and contribute some 200,000 jobs to the economy. Tourism is inextricably tied up with air transportation. Globally air transportation is the most widely used mode for tourist travel.

Tourism is a major industry both in terms of domestic tourism and from international visitations.There has been a sea change in the economy of the state over the past 25 years as tourism has produced a shift away from agriculture.

The aviation industry itself generates a significant amount of direct income for Florida through the provision of scheduled and charter passenger services and cargo operations, as well as indirectly through support services. These jobs tend to be relatively high-income. Tourists arriving by air contribute to the country's economy not only through their expenditures on air transportation, but also through spending on hotels, car rentals, meals, and entertainment.

Vacation and other leisure travelers are far more price-sensitive than business travelers. For example in 2001 37,312,000 tourists arrived in Florida by air, spending an average of $159.30 per day over a 5.3-night stay. This gives a total income of $31.5 billion associated directly with the travel industry.Application of a multiplier yields the full importance to the Florida economy. Regional Economic Models Inc. (REMI) analysis of Florida indicates a multiplier of about 1.35. Another study by Impact Analysis for Planning (IMPLAN) uses a somewhat lower multiplier. For our purposes a multiplier of 1.3 is used to give a total direct and indirect income associated with tourism of $41 million. To convert this income data into job equivalents, it is assumed that the average income for a travel-related employeein 2001 was $45,000 and for a non-travel, non-agriculture employee in 2001 was $35,000.

This is compared to actual figures of $42,866 and $32,035 respectively in 1999 and is thus a conservative estimate regarding the employment multiplier effect.To test the sensitivity of this situation to a reduction in aviation taxation, assumptions are necessary regarding the elasticities of demand. Many studies have adopted elasticities of between -1.5 and -1.7 for leisure travel; here, a conservative figure of -1.5 is used. Business travel, which constituted about 20 percent of air trips in 2001, is less sensitive to airfare variations. An elasticity of -0.9 is thus adopted. To make use of the elasticity in looking at taxation effects, it is necessary to represent any tax change as a percentage of the total ticket price. Since there is no breakdown of journey trips (direct or indirect) a number of alternatives are explored.

A similar approach is used regarding the average fare that is paid. This may be considered high for leisure routes, but because the proportional effects of most taxes fall with the fare level, this will in effect dampen any estimate of the implications of fare reductions. The number of direct, single-connection, and multiple-connection trips is not known. For simplicity the scenarios explored assume that all trips are of a single type for a particular tax change. It is a relatively simple matter to adjust the outcomes to allow for different proportions by trip category. Finally, a lower airfare resulting from reduced taxes on airlines not only will generate new traffic, but also will divert some traffic from alternative modes. Simply focusing on air travel provides a gross impact figure.

To estimate a net impact, it is necessary to consider the cross-elasticity of demand between auto travel and air travel. Data on this is sparse except for short-distance trips where substitution is more likely. The studies that do exist indicate cross-elasticities between air and automobile of about -0.3 for short-trips.While much of the visitor traffic into Florida is medium and long distance, this parameter is used here for both leisure and business travel, even though it is likely to inject downward bias into the positive effects of any aviation tax change.

MODAL COMPARISON

Examination of the tax burden on the airline industry requires a point of reference. In this section, passenger airline taxation is compared to the taxation levels of competitive modes of transportation, namely auto and rail. The distortionary effects of tax policy are especially harmful to the global economy when their implementation disrupts normal competition between industries. The airline industry is highly competitive with both trains and cars for intercity travel. Travelers, regardless of trip purpose, select their mode of transport based on a number of factors, including price, convenience, time, and comfort. The final price of travel includes the associated taxes and fees, creating a bias in the market toward auto and rail as opposed to air travel. Additionally, high taxes can result in diminished service levels or no service at all by putting downward pressure on yields and thus reducing profitability. This hurts consumers by making travel less convenient and more time consuming.

Examining the post-9/11 decline in airline traffic helps illustrate this point; an additional segment fee along with increased security hassles led to disproportionate declines in short-haul air traffic and diversion to auto travel.One carrier in particular has been very vocal in its efforts to illustrate the impact of high aviation taxes and fees on service levels. In the summer of 2002, WestJet, a low-fare and low-cost Canadian airline, ran a promotion offering "a ridiculous $3 one way fare for seats on two short-haul routes: Calgary-Edmonton and Hamilton-Ottawa. After factoring in taxes and fees, a prospective customer buying a $6 round-trip base fare ultimately paid $89 and $82, respectively, for the two markets after taxes and fees were included. WestJet wanted "to clearly show the impact these extra charges have on the wallets of Canadians" and commented that "these ridiculous taxes and fees charged to customers are discouraging people from choosing air travel as a mode of transportation on the ultra-short haul routes, and we hope Canadians will join us to voice their opinion on this situation." By transferring revenue away from air carriers to the government, high taxes and fees curtail route profitability.

Carriers are faced with the prospect of passing tax and fee increases to their customers and/or absorbing them. Given the increasingly elastic nature of air travel, price increases tend to cause market demand to shrink while cost increases negatively impact the bottom line.

Airline tax rates vary according to the itinerary, since many taxes and fees are imposed per segment. This type of taxation disproportionately affects lower airfares and multi-stop trips. For instance, taxes on the Los Angeles-Las Vegas market, primarily a leisure market, compose 24 percent of the total airfare, while taxes on the business-oriented Philadelphia-Pittsburgh market make up only 12 percent of a ticket. Intercity rail transit has no tax burden at all. In fact, there are substantial ongoing subsidies offered by the federal government to Amtrak, further distorting the market for intercity travel. Taxation on auto travel is relatively minor, as most highways are free of tolls. As a result, the total tax burden for drivers and passengers is far lower than that of air travelers. To further illustrate the inequitable tax burden facing air travelers, compare a family of four on a leisure trip from Los Angeles to Las Vegas.

The nature of air transportation superficially makes it a convenient subject of indirect taxation. As a highrevenue (though not high-profit) sector with relatively few suppliers, tax collection is relatively inexpensive and convenient for the Treasury. And as an industry air transport is politically vulnerable, lacking any large voting block to protect its interests.

There is also an ingrained common perception, largely misplaced today-after 25 years of economic deregulation and with the widespread availability of the services of low-cost air carriers-that taxation of air transportation constitutes a tax on a luxury good. This is simply not true. Today over 40 percent of airline trips are taken to visit friends and relatives and over 25 percent occur on low-cost carriers. Nevertheless, over the years a veritable kitchen sink of taxes has been imposed on America's airlines, in addition to the generic corporate taxes levied in the United States. These taxes have risen substantially over time, creating a burden that has not been more broadly shared by U.S. industries. By 2000, the airline contribution to U.S. excise tax revenues had climbed to 14 percent, up from just four percent in 1971. These special aviation taxes are imposing an excess burden on airlines and, ultimately, adversely affect not only the commercial

viability of many carriers but also the vitality of the
nation's economy and the social welfare of its citizens. This
is not to say that the airlines should be exempt from
contributing to an efficient taxation regime-rather, it is a
matter of equity and structure.

High taxation on air travel produces deleterious social
and economic outcomes, namely:

— reducing one or more aviation taxes would yield
additional employment in regions especially
dependent on aviation, such as tourism-rich Florida;

— the business community is adversely affected by high
taxes, especially highly aviation-dependent industries
such as high-tech and tourism; and

— for taxation on air travel to surpass materially taxation
on other modes of intercity travel-specifically auto and
rail-is inequitable and contrary to sound public policy.

The current aviation tax structure is causing measurable
harm to the national economy. A more rational federal
aviation tax regime-in scope, scale, and structure-would
be far more likely to stimulate growth and employment
in key sectors whose fate is closely tied to air services.
While this should be of immediate interest to tourism- and
high-tech-dependent communities and constituencies, it
should also generate additional tax revenue-to help offset
reduced aviation tax revenue-for the General Fund of the
Treasury as the growth of "ripple" industries accelerates.

The existing taxation of airlines, while often
administratively convenient and politically expedient, is
not efficient, as it is a tax on an intermediate service rather
than on final consumption. To fully reap the demonstrable
economic benefits of commercial air transportation, airlines
must be treated as economic assets rather than as a source
of sumptuary taxation. Air travel should not be treated as
a luxury good, but as a necessary and normal service
consumed by all strata of society. While in the past, airline

travel may have largely been the prerogative of the wealthy, commercial air travel is now a mode of transportation used by ordinary people and should be taxed accordingly.

When considering the taxation of airlines, full cognizance should be taken of aviation's role in facilitating the nation's external trade. The economy is increasingly part of a global marketplace, and airlines are a major contributor to the nation's global competitive position. But the current regime of aviation taxation hinders the performance of airlines in larger international markets, ultimately hurting the trade balance and eroding overall revenues.

Airlines should pay the economic costs of resources that they consume. The claim, however, that some elements of aviation taxation represent a "user charge" or "user fee" is difficult to substantiate. The taxes do not provide the incentives associated with fees nor do they act as indications of where capacity needs to be varied. Airlines often pay for items that are of no use to them. Airlines should pay directly for the inputs that they use and not pay arbitrary "user fees" that bear no relation to the economic costs involved. Similarly, the burden of taxation is not efficiently distributed between the various types of air transportation infrastructure users. General aviation, which is used almost exclusively by high-income travelers, makes extensive use of aviation infrastructure and creates considerable congestion within the system. Policymakers should reassess-indeed reallocate-the relative burdens of taxation on commercial aviation and general aviation, as well as public use, to ensure that the latter pays its fair, proportionate share.

Many twenty-first century industries, such as tourism and high-tech activities, rely disproportionately upon air transportation. These are often the industries that enjoy high growth and will continue to contribute income and employment to the nation's economy. These industries make considerable use of air transportation and high levels of taxation impede their growth. The taxation of airlines should be designed so as not to stymie the potential of dynamic industries important to American prosperity. When considering taxation of airlines, due account should be taken of the negative effects of diverting passengers to more dangerous forms of transportation.

After their initial imposition in the World War II era, aviation taxes later served to derive revenue from what was then-in the 1950s and 1960s, considered a luxury good. In the early 1970s, policymakers and airlines agreed on a new rationale for aviation taxes - to develop and maintain the nation's airport and airway infrastructure. But subsequent years added a patchwork of expanded taxes and fees, without commensurate expansion of aviation infrastructure. In the 1980s, 1990s, and early 2000s, Congress and federal agencies levied new charges for everything from general deficit reduction, to homeland security, to environmental protection, to the subsidization of noncommercial airports and operations, along with pertinent inefficiencies in the relevant regulatory agencies.

AIR TRANSPORTATION TAXES IN UNITED STATES

Much of the current structure of aviation taxation in the United States dates back to the passage of the Airport and Airway Development Act and the Airport and Airway Revenue Act of 1970. Air traffic had been growing rapidly and the forecasters anticipated continued growth. These acts aimed to provide a more solid basis for the financing of the nation's air transportation infrastructure. The Airport and Airway Development Act authorized federal funds for airport development over five years and for acquiring, establishing, and improving air-navigation facilities.

The Airport and Airway Trust Fund was established to be financed by the collection of aviation-related excise taxes, including the existing tax on aviation fuel (which dated back to the Revenue Act of 1932) and passenger tickets (dating back to the Revenue Act of 1941) the revenues from which had gone into the General Fund. New taxes were introduced on international passenger tickets, cargo waybills, and annual aircraft registration.

The Airport Improvement Act of 1982 came in as the Trust Fund had run its course and funds could no longer be transferred to it.The 1982 Act re-established the Fund and placed money in it. It allowed expenditures for operating and maintaining air-navigation facilities and, in addition, for carrying through noise-compatibility programs. In 1990 the Omnibus Budget Reconciliation Act increased excise taxes on the movement of passengers and cargo, and for non-commercial jet fuel. The 1997 Taxpayers Relief Act extended aviation-related excise taxes for 10 years to provide a stable source of funding for the Trust Fund, and the tax structure for passengers and cargo was modified and made more complex by, for example, combining flight-segment fees with fare-based taxes. Taxes were added on sales of frequent flyer miles by airlines to credit card companies and other companies that provide miles as an incentive to their customers. Of conceptual importance, the aviation fuel-tax revenue was removed from the General Fund and instead deposited to the Airport and Airway Trust Fund.

Throughout the 1990s there were some adjustments to tax rates, but the system substantively remained unchanged until the enactment of the Wendell H. Ford Aviation Investment and Reform Act for the 21Century ("AIR-21") in 2000. This legislation ensured that revenues going into the Airport and Airway Trust Fund would be used for the purposes intended.It increased the tax revenue flows available and increased the maximum that could be spent annually on a large airport. It also gave guaranteed funding to general aviation airports. The events of September 11, 2001, affected the Trust Fund in the sense that airlines under the Air Transportation Safety and System Stabilization Act of 2001 could postpone payments for a defined period.

Levels of Taxation

There are thus currently four main taxes and fees levied on domestic airfares: the federal ticket tax, the federal flight-segment tax, the passenger facility charge, and the federal security service fee. These are described in greater detail below. Since the federal ticket and flight-segment taxes are essentially two components of one tax, they are described together.

Federal ticket tax and flight-segment tax

The federal ticket tax and the federal flight-segment tax are paid into the Airport and Airway Trust Fund. This trust fund finances congressional appropriations to cover "those obligations of the U.S......which are attributable to planning, research and development, construction, or operation and maintenance of air traffic control, air navigation, communications, or supporting services for the airway system". Together they accounted for $6.3 billion in 2002, or 62 percent of the total revenue of the Trust Fund.

The federal ticket tax (FTT) is equal to 7.5 percent of the base fare. The federal segment tax (FST) was $3 per flight-segment in 2002 and 2003 (Internal Revenue Code of 1986). A built-in inflation adjustment raised the segment tax to $3.10 in 2004 and $3.20 in 2005.Passenger Facility Charge The Passenger Facility Charge (PFC) was instituted as a means for assisting airports with air carrier service to "finance eligible airport-related projects, including making payments for debt service." It is imposed by individual airports to supplement funds available from Airport Improvement Program (AIP) grants to assist in airport development and expansion.

Over time more airports have imposed the PFC and there has been a general drift upward in the fee that they elect to charge. There are local and regional variations in the levels. PFCs are collected by airlines at the time a ticket is purchased and the funds that are raised are transferred directly to the appropriate airports. PFCs have provided a steadily rising flow of revenue for the airports that levy them since their introduction.

Federal Decurity Service Fee

The federal security service fee (FSSF) or "September 11Fee," created under the 2001 Aviation and Transportation Security Act, is the most recently charge and was a direct reaction to the events of September 11, 2001. The legislation authorized a $2.50 tax per enplanement, limited to a maximum of two segments per one-way trip. Consequently, the highest possible security fee paid by a passenger on a domestic round-trip ticket is $10. Collection of the security service fee began February 1, 2002.

Other taxes

Numerous other taxes support the Airport and Airway Trust Fund, including the international arrival tax, the international departure tax, and federal aviation fuel taxes. At the more local level, individual states levy taxes, often considerable, on such things as fuel. Florida, for example, levels a $0.069 per gallon tax, Hawaii a $0.01 per gallon tax, and Colorado a $0.04 per gallon tax, on jet fuel. Some of these revenues are used as matches to be combined with monies from federal government grants as part of the AIP.

There may also be taxes levied on airport facilities themselves (e.g., car parks).

Additionally, foreign nations impose taxes and fees on U.S. carriers engaged in international operations. These can be numerous and varied, but do not apply to domestic travel. In most cases they apply to services rather than airlines and are thus paid by both the foreign carrier and the U.S. carrier that serve a particular route. The burden of taxation on airlines also includes traditional corporate taxes-amounting to about $5.4 billion in 2000-and numerous local taxes on fuel, property, sales, and franchises. The Air Transport Association estimated that in 2000 these amounted to an additional $1.5 billion.

Overall Level of Taxation

Because many of the taxes paid by airlines are neither related to flight lengths nor directly to other convenient physical parameters it is difficult to identify the "average tax burden" that confronts any airline and, ultimately, any passenger.The effective tax rates vary according to the nature of the passenger's itinerary and base fare. The burden is heaviest on those making shorter trips involving multiple connections.

The result of the current structure of aviation-related taxes is that a flow of funds from a diversity of such taxes goes into the Airport and Airway Trust Fund and are then spent on a variety of airport and airway items. Strictly the revenues go into the General Fund and are then transferred to the Trust Fund. The Airport and Airway Trust Fund covers 100 percent of Federal Aviation Administration (FAA) airport grants-in-aid; facilities and equipment; and research, engineering, and development. It also helps support over 75 percent of FAA's operations and maintenance budget.

Demand for Travel Airfares

The 1978 Airline Deregulation Act considerably changed the ways in which airlines set their fares. Rather than there being a single cost-based coach fare set by regulators with a premium being charged for first class, airlines were given the freedom to set prices so as to meet market conditions. The removal of market-entry constraints meant that fare setting was now done in a highly competitive, market environment. The result of this was a significant reduction in the average fares, albeit with some variation according to route length and service class.

Facilitated by the advent of computer reservation systems, deregulation also saw the introduction of "yield management" by many carriers, using information gained from bookings to maximize revenue per flight. More recent widespread adoption of the Internet has seen a significant increase in electronic ticketing and the expansion of traditional ticket distribution channels.This ticketing method considerably reduces costs for the airlines, but also makes it much easier for passengers to look for the cheapest type of ticket commensurate with their travel needs.

International fares in contrast, remained relatively tightly controlled, despite official initiatives from 1979, being set administratively under bilateral air service agreements with partner countries. The gradual move to Open Skies regimes from the early 1990s has removed, largely within a web of liberalized bilateral agreements, this type of barrier to fare setting, and also to market entry, and the majority of international routes served by U.S. airlines are now within competitive markets.

These changes, while demonstrably beneficial to U.S. citizens, complicate analysis, management and public policy considerably. For example, the move away from regulated, rate-of-return regulation removed any guarantee of a stable income flow that would allow for a steady stream of tax revenues. The move toward Internet distribution and the subsequent increase in pricing transparency has transferred more pricing power to customers and has reduced the market power of airlines and removed one mechanism that allowed them to recover costs.

Performance of Airline Industry

The airline industry provides inputs into a variety of other activities - including business, leisure and visiting family. The demand for air transportation is de facto a derived demand. In the short-term the demand for airline services is thus sensitive to the demands for these final activities. This in particular makes it highly sensitive to trade-cycle effects. In addition, it is a highly competitive industry. The nature of this competition and its intensity is reflected in the relative frequency of entry and exit of airlines. It also extends across several dimensions including direct competition on many routes, and indirect competition between the networks of services offered by carriers and the multiplicity of indirect routings that exist between cities.

Financial Situation of Airlines

As a generalization, the greater the degree of market power that an individual enterprise has, the easier it is for it to pass at least part of the tax on to its customers. In a highly competitive market with few scale economies, however, you ultimately get higher prices and lower (or poorer quality) output as a result of imposing a tax. In the airlines' case, in the short-term individual carriers may try to absorb part of the tax to retain a competitive edge. But with all carriers doing this, and in the absence of any significant profits at the outset, inevitably some carriers will leave the market.

The removal or reduction of a tax from a competitive market with no entry or exit barriers has the opposite effect. Lowering of taxes may initially see airlines trying to earn economic profits but this merely attracts new capacity (either from incumbents expanding services or from new entrants) with the result that fares are forced down again to cost and the level of service for potential passengers rises. The 1978 Airline Deregulation Act removed fare controls and allowed airlines conforming to safety, environmental and other social criteria to provide service. The result is that the U.S. market is a highly competitive network business. Not only do many direct routes have a number of suppliers but there is also competition from connecting services offered via hubs. On shorter-haul routes, air service competes with the automobile and rail, with Amtrak also offering subsidized competition in a limited number of corridors. Air cargo suppliers not only compete with each other but also with railroads and trucks in some segments of their markets.

Historically, U.S. airlines have cumulatively lost several billion dollars. The operating margins for the industry have varied but the average return is well below that expected of an industry with the characteristics of air transportation. As with any industry, variability in the quality of management is accompanied by disparities in the financial performance of individual suppliers. The financial picture of U.S. airlines, however, reflects more of an industry-wide issue than one of a set of individual managerial failures. In a competitive market such as air transportation there is an acute sensitivity to prices of inputs and to the adverse implications of imposing an excess burden on suppliers. Under those commercial circumstances, one can safely conclude that increased taxation will worsen the financial results of the collective supplier community.

Elasticities of demand

To conduct any assessment of the effects of taxation on the financial condition of airlines, and on the economy more generally, one must have insight into the effects that taxes have on the demand for air services. The fare elasticity of demand for air travel indicates the sensitivity of revenue to the level of fare being charged.Specifically it looks at the proportional change in the number of units sold against a proportional change in unit price. "Unit" price elasticity means that a 10 percent rise in price results in a 10 percent fall in units sold - thus, a neutral effect on revenues.

When the demand is inelastic, the marginal revenue effect associated with any price fall is negative; conversely, if the segment of a demand curve is fare elastic it means that any reduction in fare will lead to an increase in total revenue. There are various ways of calculating the fare elasticities of demand, and the task of estimation is far from easy. There are estimates of arc elasticities that look at a discrete change in a fare level and there are point elasticities that focus on a marginal change.The elasticities may be calculated using time series data for a single carrier or market, in which case the underlying assumption is that the result is a short-run elasticity, whereas cross-section calculations of the implications of a particular fare change across several markets at a point bin time offer estimates of long-run elasticities.

Elasticity parameter estimates may be sensitive to the type of calculation procedure used and to the way in which other factors influencing demand are treated. The use of yield management by airlines, whereby there is no single fare charged in a cabin, adds to the complexity of calculation.

10

AIRLINE DEREGULATION

The airline industry has undergone significant change since the late 1970s. Airlines that predated deregulation, called legacy airlines, emerged from regulation with significant structural costs, including labor contracts that funded defined benefit pension plans. Legacy airlines dominated the industry during the 1980s and 1990s because of their size and a variety of business practices that made it difficult for new entrant airlines to compete. Industry employment, compensation, and efficiency have all grown since deregulation.

However, with the major industry downturn that began in 2000, new entrant airlines-unburdened by many of the structural costs of legacy airlines-were better able to compete for passengers with low fares and have gained market share. By 2003, low-cost airlines served 2,304 out of the top 5,000 city-pair domestic markets, representing a presence in markets available to almost 85 percent of all passengers.

In response to sizeable financial losses after 2000, both United and US Airways entered bankruptcy and terminated their pension plans, costing the Pension Benefit Guaranty Corporation (PBGC) nearly $10 billion and beneficiaries more than $5 billion. In 2005, two other legacy airlines entered bankruptcy, leaving their pension plans in doubt. Only two airlines, American and Continental, still have active defined benefit pension plans in place.

As predicted by the framers of deregulation, airline markets have become more competitive and fares have fallen since deregulation. For consumers, airfares have fallen in real terms since 1980 while service has generally improved. Overall, median fares have declined in real terms by nearly 40 percent since 1980. However, fares in shorter-distance and less-traveled city-pair markets have not fallen as much as fares in longer-distance and heavily-trafficked markets. While the competition brought about by deregulation likely played a significant role in bringing down fares, the extent to which these changes are directly attributable to deregulation as opposed to other factors, such as advances in technology or economic factors, is difficult to isolate.

Various studies have attributed substantial consumer benefits to deregulation, but estimating the size of this benefit requires making several assumptions about what fares would be if they were still regulated. More passengers are flying between more city-pair markets, but that, on average, passengers are making more connections to reach their destinations. Service improvements have not been as evident in smaller markets as in larger ones. Since 1980, city-pair markets have generally become more competitive even while passenger traffic became more concentrated. Longer-distance and more heavily traveled markets in particular have become more competitive, with the average number of competitors growing from 2.2 per market in 1980 to 3.5 in 2005. Some indicators of other aspects of service quality, such as rates of on-time arrival or lost luggage, suggest that service quality may have eroded somewhat over the past few years.

Reregulation of airline entry and fares would likely reverse much of the benefits that consumers have gained and would not save airline pensions. Our analysis of fares and service since deregulation provides evidence that consumers have benefited from lower fares since the airlines were deregulated. Since deregulation, competition has generally increased, traffic has expanded, and fares have declined. The primary dislocations that have occurred since deregulation-loss of service to some communities and the decline of legacy airlines' finances and pensions-are the result of competitive market forces. Therefore, attempting to resolve the dislocations that have occurred for some small communities or the loss of pension benefits for some airline workers by restraining these same forces could reverse some of the gains that have accrued.

If the government determines that service to small communities is inadequate, then direct subsidies might be a more efficient solution than reregulating the industry and diminishing the benefits gained by a majority of consumers. The financial distress of some legacy airlines, while regrettable (especially for airline employees), was not unanticipated, and is evidence of a functioning market in which lower-cost airlines have emerged, generally benefiting consumers with lower fares. These financial problems also caused several legacy airlines to freeze or terminate their defined benefit pension plans, leaving only two airlines with active plans.

The airlines' pension problems are no different from the pension problems occurring throughout the economy and can be traced to broad economic factors, poor management decisions, and inadequate pension regulation. Therefore, broad pension reform that is comprehensive in scope and balanced in effect would more logically address problems with airline pensions than more sweeping airline industry regulation, which could undo the benefits that deregulation has achieved.

Industrywide regulation of the U.S. airline industry began in 1938 in response to congressional concern over safety, airlines' financial health, and perceived inequities between airlines and other regulated forms of transportation. The Civil Aeronautics Act of 1938 (P.L. 706) applied to interstate operations of U.S. airlines and gave the Civil Aeronautics Authority, redesignated as the Civil Aeronautics Board (CAB) in 1940, authority to regulate which airlines operated on each route and what fares they could charge. Airlines could not add or abandon routes or change fares without CAB approval.

CAB also limited the number of airlines in the industry. In 1938, the interstate U.S. airline industry consisted of 16 "trunk" airlines, but this number contracted to 10 by 1974, despite 79 applications from new airlines to initiate service. Competition was limited on a route to one airline unless the CAB determined that demand was sufficient to support an additional airline. Airfares were based on a complex cost-based formula used by the CAB, though the exact formulas and process varied over the life of the CAB. Generally, though, airlines during this time had little incentive to reduce costs, since each was assured a fixed rate of return. As a result, the competition that existed among airlines was largely based on the quality of service. Airlines operated largely a point-to-point system, more similar to railroads than the airline networks that we know today.

Airlines have traditionally relied on union labor, and labor relations have been covered by the Railway Labor Act since 1936. The union bargaining structure that developed within the airline industry has been highly decentralized and separated by craft (e.g., pilots, mechanics, etc.). Before deregulation, unions and airline management engaged in carrier-by-carrier bargaining whereby the last contract signed by one carrier generally served as the starting point for the next airline (known as "pattern bargaining"). During regulation, labor relations were generally good because CAB's fare-setting allowed airlines to pass increased labor costs on to passengers. Airlines' bargaining power was enhanced by the Mutual Aid Pact, a strike insurance plan created in 1958, through which a struck airline was compensated by nonstruck airlines based on increases in traffic the latter received during a strike. The Mutual Aid Pact was eliminated with deregulation, thereby enhancing airline labor's power in contract negotiations.

INTENTION OF AIRLINE DEREGULATION

The Airline Deregulation Act phased out federal control over airline pricing and routes. Airline deregulation was premised on an expectation that an unregulated industry would attract entry and increase competition among airlines, thereby benefiting consumers with lower fares and improved service. The experience of unregulated (i.e., state-regulated) intrastate service in Texas and California provided support for this expectation. Moreover, prior to deregulation, industry analysts-on the basis of conventional economic reasoning-expected that opportunities for increased competition would increase the number of airlines operating in many markets, thereby lowering fares and expanding service.

The Airline Deregulation Act established specific goals of encouraging competition by attracting new entrant airlines and allowing existing airlines to expand. According to the act, competition was expected to lower fares and expand service, the chief aims of deregulation.At the same time, Congress recognized that deregulation could lead to economic dislocations for some communities and workers as service patterns adjusted and airlines entered and exited markets and the industry overall. As a result, the EAS program and the EPP were established.

The EAS program was put into place to guarantee that small communities served by commercial airlines before deregulation would maintain a minimal level of scheduled air service. Department of Transportation (DOT) currently subsidizes commuter airlines to serve approximately 150 rural communities across the country that otherwise would not receive any scheduled air service. According to DOT, EAS subsidizes 39 communities in Alaska and 115 more in the rest of the United States. The EAS budget ranged from about $100 million early in the program down to about $25 million, before rising in recent years to $100 million. In Fiscal Year 2006, EAS was funded at $109 million.

EPP was created, first, to compensate airline workers who lost their jobs or received lower pay as a result of bankruptcies or major contractions whose major cause was airline deregulation and, second, to grant such workers first-hire rights. However, the Department of Labor delayed the establishment of regulations to administer these rights, Congress did not appropriate funds to compensate displaced employees, and airlines fought the requirements in court. On August 7, 1998, the statute authorizing the EPP was repealed.No compensation was ever provided to displaced employees, and the first-hire right was never enforced.

While the practice of setting of airline entry and rates was deregulated, the federal government is still involved in many facets of the airline industry, including many aspects that affect the economics of the industry. For example, the federal government still influences financing and investment decisions affecting the nation's aviation infrastructure, including airports and air navigation systems. In addition to the various taxes and user fees on commercial airline tickets, which averaged 15.5 percent of the base fare in 2002, the federal government also provides support from its general fund for Federal Aviation Administration (FAA) operations. In 2007, the Airport and Airways Trust Fund, which finances the nation's aviation infrastructure, will be up for renewal. The federal government also provided commercial airlines with $7.4 billion in financial assistance and $1.6 billion in loan guarantees for six airlines as a result of the September 11, 2001, terrorist attacks. Finally, PBGC has assumed almost $12 billion in net airline pension obligations since 1991.

CHANGES IN AIRLINE INDUSTRY AFTER DEREGULATION

The airline industry has undergone significant change since the late 1970s. Air travel, and along with it industry revenues and expenses, have tripled since 1978. However, industry profits have become increasingly cyclic, with the most recent downturn leading to almost $28 billion in operating losses since 2001. Airline employee compensation grew following deregulation, even though many studies have found that employees earned a premium under regulation. Nevertheless, employee compensation as a share of total expenses has declined, especially in recent years.

During regulation, airlines operated almost as regulated monopolies, encountering little competition and facing little pressure to restrain costs because fares were based on the airlines' costs plus a fixed rate of return. Following deregulation, legacy airlines were able to stave off new entrant competition through various operating barriers, -imposed take-off and landing times at congested airports (slot controls), perimeter rules at Washington Reagan National Airport, and airlines' exclusive-use control of gate leases; and business practices, such as frequent flyer programs and ticket distribution systems. The market downturn that began in 2000 exposed legacy airlines' precarious financial condition, allowing low-cost airlines the opportunity to compete more aggressively. Owing to financial instability since deregulation, airlines operating in bankruptcy have become more common, but bankruptcy protection has not adversely affected nonbankrupt airlines. More troubling has been the use of bankruptcy to terminate defined-benefit pension plans, costing the PBGC and airline employees billions of dollars. Only two airlines still offer defined benefit pension plans.

The U.S. airline industry has expanded threefold since deregulation.the consumption of airline travel as measured by revenue passenger miles (RPM) grew from 188 billion RPMs in 1978 to 584 billion RPMs in 2005, while airline capacity grew at a similar pace-from 306 billion available seat miles (ASM) in 1978 to 758 billion ASMs in 2005. Over the same period, revenue passenger enplanementsincreased from 254 million in 1978 to 670 million in 2005.

Owing to the growth of air travel, U.S. airlines' revenues grew almost fourfold in real terms. However, expenses also grew at a similar pace, sometimes outpacing industry revenues. While profits were relatively stable under regulation, earnings have been increasingly cyclical since deregulation. One explanation for this cyclicality is that, with revenues closely tied to the business cycle, high fixed costs for aircraft, and a rigid and costly labor structure, outside shocks-such as the September 11, 2001, attacks or high fuel prices-make it difficult for the industry to adjust its capacity. The industry has incurred operating losses of nearly $28 billion since 2001, most of this by legacy airlines.These airlines have compensated by taking on additional debt, using all (or nearly all) of their assets as collateral and limiting future access to capital.

AIRLINE SALARIES, COMPENSATION, AND EFFICIENCY

There have been significant changes to airline employee compensation, employment, and productivity since deregulation. Prior to deregulation, labor was highly unionized and wage demands were typically met.

Regulation allowed for increases in labor costs to be passed on to consumers through the regulated fare system. Several studies have estimated that airline wages were greater under regulation than they would have been in a competitive deregulated market.Even so, industry growth, barriers to entry, and union bargaining strength allowed labor to protect its compensation following deregulation.

Since 1978, airline industry salaries and total compensation experienced real increases, though with some decline since 2002. Inflation-adjusted benefits per employee grew on average from $14,703 in 1979 to $24,852 in 2004, a real increase of almost 70 percent. Meanwhile, inflation-adjusted salaries per employee grew from $52,295 in 1979 to $54,848 in 2004 on average, a real increase of less than 5 percent. Despite this increase in compensation costs, employee compensation as a share of total operating costs has declined since deregulation, especially since 2002.

This decline in compensation costs as a share of total operating expense is attributable to falling employment levels, to large increases in capacity, and increases in other costs (especially for fuel). Employment began to decline with the industry downturn that began in 2000. As a result, measures of overall industry efficiency increased significantly. This is attributable to efficiency gains by legacy airlines during and under the threat of bankruptcy, and to more efficient low-cost carriers providing more capacity than previously.

Following deregulation, legacy airlines were considerably larger and better financed than the host of small new airlines that entered the market place. Most of the new entrant airlines during the 1980s and 1990s failed. Large legacy airlines were generally able to retain market share despite new entrant airlines because of operating barriers-such as slot controls-and business practices-such as frequent flyer programs-that gave them competitive advantages. Larger and better-capitalized legacy airlines seeking to increase market share acquired weaker airlines.

Since the industry downturn that began in 2000, there has been a shift in the airline industry: a weakening of the financial condition of legacy airlines and an increasing market share for low-cost carriers. The consequences of an overburdened cost structure for legacy airlines became apparent after 2000 when demand fell, especially demand from premium-fare business travelers. Low-cost airlines, which generally did not have these cost structures, have been able to increase their market share, while legacy airlines have struggled to bring their costs down.

Low-cost airlines increased their presence in the top 5,000 domestic city-pair markets by 44.5 percent; from 1,594 markets in 1998 to 2,304 markets in 2003.In 1998, low-cost airlines operated in 31.5 percent of markets served by legacy airlines, providing a low-cost airline alternative to 72.5 percent of passengers. By 2003, low-cost airlines competed directly with legacy airlines in 45.5 percent of markets served by legacy airlines, serving 84.6 percent of passengers in the top 5,000 markets. While legacy airlines began to reduce their operating costs starting in 2001, they did so through capacity reductions and were not able to reduce their unit costs vis-à-vis low-cost airlines that were adding capacity. Legacy airlines could not survive with continued losses. In 2005, two legacy airlines entered bankruptcy and are currently attempting to reorganize.

ISSUE OF AIRLINE BANKRUPTCY

Bankruptcy has been endemic to the airline industry since deregulation, with 162 bankruptcy filings since 1978, owing to the fundamental financial weaknesses of the airline industry. Despite the prevalence of bankruptcy, however, there was no evidence that bankruptcy harmed the airline industry by contributing to overcapacity or by underpricing.

DECLINE OF AIRFARES

Airfares have fallen in real terms over time, with round-trip median fares almost 40 percent lower since 1980. However, fares in short-distance markets and "thin" markets have not fallen as much as those for longer distances or in heavily traveled markets. Price dispersion-that is, the extent to which passengers in the same city-pair market pay different fares-has also declined since 2003, likely indicating consumers' unwillingness to pay the very high fares airlines were able to charge in the late 1990s.

The extent to which these benefits are attributable to deregulation as opposed to other factors, such as advances in technology, is uncertain. Various studies have attributed significant consumer benefit to deregulation, but estimating this benefit depends on several major assumptions and is not free of controversy. The decline in fares coincided with a growth in passenger traffic and increased competition over the period. While large communities and markets have experienced large gains in the number of passengers and service, as well as increased competition, small communities and markets have experienced much smaller gains. On average, however, the number of competitors in city-pair markets grew from 2.2 in 1980 to 3.5 in 2005.

There is a substantial decreases in median fares since 1980, with an overall decrease of nearly 40 percent for median round-trip fares since that time. In recent years, passengers flying long distances or in medium to large markets have paid much lower fares as compared with 1980 fares, while those flying in smaller markets or over shorter distances today have seen a smaller reduction in fares as compared with 1980 fares. Finally, the difference between the fares paid by customers flying within the same routes began to decline in 2003, after increasing in the years following deregulation.

Overall, median round-trip fares have declined 38 percent since 1980, falling from $414 to $256.The largest decreases occurred in the late 1980s, but the overall trends have continued down in subsequent years.Median fares have converged when compared by the distance traveled since deregulation. In 1980, median fares ranged from $680 for trips longer than 1,500 miles to $230 for trips of 250 miles or less- reflecting the pricing structure in place under regulation, which linked fares to costs while subsidizing shorter routes.since that time, however, fares have converged toward the low end of this range, with the longest trips now averaging just $326, a drop of 52 percent. Median fares for the shortest trips, in contrast, have not fallen as much. For trips of 250 miles or less, median fares have fallen 13 percent to $201.

The size of the market has also affected how fares have changed since deregulation.The smallest markets continue to have the highest average fares, and have seen the smallest reduction in these fares. In 1980, passengers flying in the smallest markets paid $412 on average for their tickets, while those flying in the largest markets paid $329. Examples of city pairs in the smallest-market category in both 1980 and 2005 include the Atlanta, Georgia-Joplin, Missouri route; and the Great Falls, Montana-Sacramento, California route. In contrast, the Boston, Massachusetts-New York, New York route; and the Chicago, Illinois-Los Angeles, California route, were in the largest-market category in both 1980 and 2005.

While median fares trended down steadily after deregulation, the differences in the prices paid by individual customers in the same city-pair market grew, most notably in the 1990s with the increased use of yieldmanagement systems by airlines.The dispersion of fares began to decline in 2003, however, when changes in the overall economy and a decline in the willingness of some passengers to pay higher fares for premium service-notably business passengers-likely combined with the increased use of the Internet for ticket purchases to reverse some of the prior increases in ticketing variation. Since then, the variability of fares has decreased, meaning that fares for most tickets sold are now generally more similar to average fares.

Many studies have estimated that consumers have benefited from deregulation. Assessments of these benefits, however, vary substantially as have the methodologies used. One approach is to calculate the difference between actual fares and a benchmark proxy measure of what fares might have been had the industry remained regulated. Any differences are then attributed to the effects of deregulation. Some studies using this approach have used the Standard Industry Fare Level (SIFL) to approximate the regulated fare and concluded that consumers as a whole have benefited from lower fares resulting from deregulation.

For example, in 2005 Rose and Borenstein compared postderegulation fares to the SIFL and estimated that 2004 fares were about 30 percent lower than what the comparative regulated fares would have been, resulting in a $5 billion savings to passengers that year.Likewise, Winston and Morrison used the same proxy in 1995 and estimated that real fares declined about 33 percent from 1976 to 1993. After adjusting the SIFL data to account for presumed productivity gains and increased load factors,they estimated that, on average, deregulation led to fares 22 percent lower than they would have been in a regulated environment, resulting in an annual savings of about $12.4 billion in 1993 dollars over the same period. While pointing to declines in overall fares, these studies also indicated that benefits have been unevenly distributed by market size and route length. In fact, those traveling on heavily traveled routes are likely to be paying less than they would have paid under a regulated system, and those flying on shorter-distance routes are likely to be paying more. Some experts have questioned the extent to which deregulation can be credited for decreases in airfares since 1978, and draw attention to the difficulty in measuring impact. First, a former CAB and DOT official, who participated in CAB route awards and fare determinations and later calculated the SIFL for DOT, points out that the fare ceilings used by CAB under regulation-calculated as the Domestic Passenger Fare Investigation (DPFI)-were more complicated than their proxies. Rose and Borenstein also acknowledged that using the SIFL as a proxy for the CAB regulated fare may be increasingly implausible, given that it is unlikely that the same cost assumptions would have been used for the 27 years following deregulation.

As a result, using the SIFL to approximate airline fares under regulation may overestimate the savings resulting from deregulation. For example, while the DPFI fare calculations took several factors into account, including depreciation and capacity, the SIFL calculations primarily consider airline costs.The former DOT official further noted that the DPFI calculations allowed for discounted fares if load factors were increased to offset the fare reduction, something not reflected by the SIFL fare. Second, some experts have pointed out that fares were already declining before deregulation, thus making it difficult to attribute changes in the industry to deregulation rather than improvements in productivity and other factors.In fact, real average fares paid per mile (yields) since 1962 do show a steady decline, reflecting both CAB fare setting flexibility and cost-savings following the introduction of jet service in the early 1960s, but without a sharp break in 1978 following the deregulation of the industry.

GROWTH OF AIRLINE MARKETS

Airline city-pair markets have become more competitive since deregulation. The average number of effective competitors (any airline that carries at least 5 percent of the traffic in that market) in any city pair increased from 2.2 in 1980 to 3.5 in 2005.By 2005, 76 percent of the city-pair markets had three or more carriers compared with 34 percent of all city-pair markets in 1980. By contrast, the percentage of city-pair markets with only one carrier decreased from 20 percent in 1980 to 5 percent in 2005. Most of the increase in competition occurred during the 1980s, just after deregulation.

Longer-distance markets are more competitive than shorter-distance markets, some of which have lost competitors since 1980. While city pairs with a distance of over 1,500 miles have seen an increase in the average number of carriers from 2.3 in 1980 to 4.2 in 2005, markets shorter than 250 miles have seen a decrease from 1.6 in 1980 to 1.4 in 2005. This difference exists in large part because longer-distance markets have more viable options for connecting over more hubs. For example, a passenger on a long-haul flight from Harrisburg, Pennsylvania, to Seattle, Washington (a distance of over 2,000 miles), would have options of connecting through six different hubs, including Cincinnati, Chicago, and Detroit. By comparison, a passenger from Harrisburg to Rochester, New York (a distance of just over 200 miles), has three viable connecting options.

CITY-PAIR MARKET

Passenger traffic, already concentrated in relatively few city-pair markets in 1980, has become more concentrated. In 1980, 80 percent of passenger traffic occurred in the largest 14.1 percent of all city-pair markets, but by 2005, that same percentage of traffic occurred in the largest 10.7 percent of all city-pair markets. While large markets have seen substantial gains in traffic, smaller markets have not, and in many cases have actually seen declines in traffic since deregulation.

The number of city-pair markets has increased modestly since 1980. Largely owing to an overall growth in traffic, the number of city pairs with at least 13 passengers in the sample per quarter (which equates to about 130 actual passengers per quarter) increased by over 3,800 city-pair markets between 1980 and 2005, from about 8,500 to over 12,300. However, few cities have gained air service since deregulation because the airport system was already largely developed at the time of deregulation, so the number of cities that could be connected would not be expected to have changed much since deregulation. Instead, many city-pair markets that could be connected did not have enough actual passengers reflected in the sample data to be counted.

Smaller communities, in general, have not experienced the same increases in traffic and air service as larger cities since deregulation-particularly in recent years, when many small cities lost service or experienced a decline in the number of departures.

The primary reason for diminished service to smaller communities is the lack of a population base to support that service. Local air traffic is directly related to both local population and employment. For small communities located close to larger cities, these demand reductions are exacerbated because local passengers drive to airports in larger cities to access better service and lower fares.

Some EAS airports serve only about 10 percent of the intercity traffic to and from their city because many travelers instead drive to alternative airports or to their destination. Small communities have not benefited from the service of low-cost carriers. Lack of service from low-cost airlines can partially explain why small cities also face relatively higher fares than larger cities do.

The average number of connections needed, at a minimum, to connect any two cities has increased since

1980. Very few citypair markets currently require two connections. The average number of connections needed to connect any two city-pair markets increased from 1.6 in 1980 to 1.7 in 2005, which is likely attributable to the development of hub-and-spoke networks to connect airline traffic. For some passengers this development has increased the number of connections needed. For example, in 1980, passengers traveling between Philadelphia, Pennsylvania, and Tulsa, Oklahoma, could fly nonstop, but by 2005 one connection was required.

While there may have been declines in nonstop connectivity for many small city-pair markets, the overall ability of passengers to connect to wider markets through hubs has likely improved. The shift from shorter-range turboprop planes to longer-range regional jets has allowed cities that are too small to support mainline jet service, but too far from hubs for turboprop service, to be connected to hubs, increasing the number of one-connection city-pair opportunities. The largest markets are generally served by nonstop service.

In 2005, 88 percent of passengers traveled in city-pair markets that included nonstop service and less than 1 percent of passengers traveled in city-pair markets that required two connections.However, because many passengers in directly connected markets may choose to fly with a connection (e.g., in exchange for a lower fare), the actual number of passengers flying without a connection is lower. For example, while passengers flying between Seattle and Tampa, Florida, could fly nonstop in 2005, they could also choose to connect through a number of hubs, including Chicago, Atlanta, and Denver, Colorado, for a number of reasons. Our data do not distinguish between passengers who flew with one or two connections out of necessity (e.g., because of no better option in their market) or voluntarily when a direct flight was available.

Reregulation of airline entry and rates would not benefit consumers and the airline industry. Although some aspects of customer service might improve, reregulation would likely reverse many of the gains made by consumers, especially lower fares. While numerous industries have been deregulated over the last 30 years, very few have been reregulated. The few instances in which an industry was reregulated stemmed from inadequate competition, such as occurred in the cable television industry after it was deregulated. Lack of competition has not been the case in the airline industry, where competition has been keen.

Consumers have benefited over the intervening years. While it is impossible to accurately calculate these gains because no regulated system exists against which to compare deregulated fares, deregulation has corresponded with increased competition in the airline industry, which has likely contributed to lower fares and a larger airline market than might have prevailed without it. Reregulating the airline industry would have ramifications reaching far beyond the fare and service effects on airline passengers and communities. For example, the higher fares for airline travel that would likely result from reregulating the industry could shift some of the nation's 670 million domestic airline passengers to other modes of transportation that are neither as safe nor efficient as air travel, and considerable infrastructure investment would be required to handle the increased demand.

Restoring service to some small communities is an insufficient reason to reregulate airline entry and rates. Small communities face a range of fundamental economic challenges in attracting and retaining commercial air service. Among these challenges is the lack of a population base or economic activity that could generate sufficient passenger demand to make service profitable to airlines. Smaller communities located near larger airports may also face reduced demand because they do not have low-cost airlines or frequent service.

Despite these challenges, smaller city-pair markets have generally experienced lower fares since deregulation-just not to the degree that the largest citypair markets have. The smallest city-pair markets have also experienced a net gain in the number of connections and in overall traffic since deregulation.

Reregulating the airline industry would not salvage airline pensions. Legacy airlines' financial problems are the result of the same competitive forces that contributed to lower fares for consumers. The demise of airlines since deregulation has been endemic to the airline industry, as more efficient airlines have taken market share from less efficient airlines. Pension losses were attributable to market forces, poor airline management and union decisions, and inadequate pension funding rules-including insufficient funding requirements and the inadequate relationship between premiums paid by plan sponsors and PBGC's exposure to financial risk. These factors also led to the termination of pensions in other industries with large legacy pension costs, such as steel. Increasing fares via government-imposed price floors similar to those that existed prior to 1978 would be an inefficient means of ensuring that airlines would generate sufficient revenues to adequately fund their pension plans, especially when most airlines no longer offer defined benefit plans.

11

AIR TRAVEL : SECURITY CONCERNS

AIR TRAVEL: HEALTH CONSIDERATIONS

Air travel, in particular over long distances, exposes passengers to a number of factors that may have an effect on their health and well-being. Passengers with pre-existing health problems are more likely to be affected and should consult their doctor or a travel medicine clinic in good time before travelling. Those receiving medical care and intending to travel by air in the near future should tell their medical adviser. Health risks associated with air travel can be minimized if the traveller plans carefully and takes some simple precautions before, during, and after the flight. An explanation of the various factors that may affect the health and well-being of air travellers follows.

Although aircraft cabins are pressurized, cabin air pressure at cruising altitude is lower than air pressure at sea level. At typical cruising altitudes in the range 11 000-12 200 metres (36 000-40 000 feet) air pressure in the cabin is equivalent to the outside air pressure at 1800-2400 metres (6000-8000 feet) above sea level. As a consequence, less oxygen is taken up by the blood (hypoxia) and gases within the body expand. The effects of reduced cabin air pressure are usually well tolerated by healthy passengers.

Cabin Air Pressure

Cabin air contains ample oxygen for healthy passengers and crew. However, because cabin air pressure is relatively low, the amount of oxygen carried in the blood is reduced compared to sea level. Passengers with certain medical conditions, in particular heart and lung disease, and blood disorders such as anaemia, may not tolerate this reduced oxygen level (hypoxia) very well. Such passengers are usually able to travel safely if arrangements are made with the airline for the provision of an additional oxygen supply during flight.

As the aircraft climbs, the decreasing cabin air pressure causes gases to expand. Similarly, as the aircraft descends, the increasing pressure in the cabin causes gases to contract. These changes may have effects where gas is trapped in the body. Gas expansion during the climb causes air to escape from the middle ear and the sinuses, usually without causing problems. This airflow can sometimes be perceived as a "popping" sensation in the ears. As the aircraft descends, air must flow back into the middle ear and sinuses in order to equalize pressure differences. If this does not take place, the ears or sinuses may feel as if they were blocked and, if the pressure is not relieved, pain can result.

Swallowing, chewing, or yawning ('clearing the ears') will usually relieve any discomfort. If the problem persists, a short forceful expiration against a pinched nose and closed mouth (Valsalva manœuvre) will usually help. For infants, feeding or giving a pacifier (dummy) to stimulate swallowing may reduce the symptoms. Individuals with ear, nose, and sinus infections should avoid flying because pain and injury may result from the inability to equalize pressure differences. If travel cannot be avoided, the use of decongestant nasal drops shortly before the flight and again before descent may be helpful.

As the aircraft climbs, expansion of gas in the abdomen can cause discomfort, although this is usually mild. Some forms of surgery, other medical treatments, or diagnostic tests, may introduce air or other gas into a body cavity. Examples include abdominal surgery or eye treatment for a detached retina. Passengers who have recently undergone such a procedure should ask a travel medicine physician or their treating physician how long they should wait before undertaking air travel.

Cabin Humidity

The humidity in aircraft cabins is low, usually less than 20% (humidity in the home is normally over 30%). Low humidity may cause skin dryness and discomfort of the eyes, mouth, nose and exposed skin but presents no risk to health. Using a skin moisturizing lotion, saline nasal spray to moisturize the nasal passages, and wearing spectacles rather than contact lenses can relieve or prevent discomfort. The low humidity does not cause dehydration and there is no need to drink extra water.

Ozone is a form of oxygen (with three, rather than two, atoms to the molecule) that occurs in the upper atmosphere and may enter the aircraft cabin together with the fresh air supply. In older aircraft, it was found that the levels of ozone in cabin air could sometimes lead to irritation of the lungs, eyes and nasal tissues. Ozone is broken down by heat and most ozone is removed by the compressors (in the aircraft engines) that provide pressurized air for the cabin. In addition, most modern long-haul jet aircraft are fitted with equipment (catalytic converters) that breaks down any remaining ozone.

Cosmic Radiation

Cosmic radiation is made up of radiation that comes from the sun and from outer space. The earth's atmosphere and magnetic field are natural shields and therefore cosmic radiation levels are lower at lower altitudes. Cosmic radiation is more intense over polar regions than over the equator because of the shape of the earth's magnetic field and the "flattening" of the atmosphere over the poles. The population is continually exposed to natural background radiation from soil, rock and building materials as well as from cosmic radiation that reaches the earth's surface. Although cosmic radiation levels are higher at aircraft cruising altitudes than at sea level, research so far has not shown any significant health effects for either passengers or crew.

Motion Sickness

Except in the case of severe turbulence, travellers by air rarely suffer from motion (travel) sickness. Those who do suffer should request a seat in the mid-section of the cabin where movements are less pronounced, and keep the motion sickness bag, provided at each seat, readily accessible. They should also consult their doctor or travel medicine physician about medication that can be taken before flight to help prevent problems.

Immobility and Circulatory Problems

Contraction of muscles is an important factor in helping to keep blood flowing through the veins, particularly in the legs. Prolonged immobility, especially when seated, can lead to pooling of blood in the legs, which in turn may cause swelling, stiffness, and discomfort.

It is known that immobility is one of the factors that may lead to the development of a blood clot in a deep vein, so-called "deep vein thrombosis", or DVT. Research has shown that DVT can occur as a result of prolonged immobility, for instance during long distance travel, whether by car, bus, train or air. The World Health

Organization (WHO) has set up a major research study to find out if there are any factors that might lead to the risk of DVT being higher for air travel than for other causes of immobility.

In most cases of DVT, the clots are small and do not cause any symptoms. The body is able to gradually break down the clot and there are no long-term effects. Larger clots may cause symptoms such as swelling of the leg, tenderness, soreness and pain. Occasionally a piece of the clot may break off and travel with the bloodstream to become lodged in the lungs. This is known as pulmonary embolism and may cause chest pain, shortness of breath and, in severe cases, sudden death. This can occur many hours or even days after the formation of the clot.

The risk of developing DVT when travelling is very small unless one or more other risk factors are present. These include:

— Previous DVT or pulmonary embolism

— History of DVT or pulmonary embolism in a close family member

— Use of oestrogen therapy-oral contraceptives "or hormone replacement therapy (HRT)

— Pregnancy

— Recent surgery or trauma, particularly to the abdomen, pelvic region or legs

— Cancer

— Some inherited blood-clotting abnormalities.

It is advisable for people with one or more of these risk factors to seek specific medical advice from their doctor or a travel medicine clinic in good time before embarking on a flight of three or more hours.

DVT occurs more commonly in older people. Some researchers have suggested that there may be a risk from smoking, obesity and varicose veins.

The risk of a passenger who does not have any of the risk factors above developing DVT as a consequence of flying is small and the benefits of most precautionary measures in such passengers are unproven and some might even result in harm. Some common-sense advice for such passengers is given below. Moving around the cabin during long flights will help to reduce any period of prolonged immobility. However, this may not always be possible and any potential health benefits must be balanced against the risk of injury that could occur if the aircraft encounters sudden and unexpected turbulence.

A sensible compromise is to walk around in the cabin, e.g. go to the bathroom, once every 2-3 hours. Many airlines also provide helpful advice on exercises that can be carried out in the seat during flight. It is thought that exercise of the calf muscles can stimulate the circulation, reduce discomfort, fatigue and stiffness, and it may reduce the risk of developing DVT. Hand luggage should not be placed where it restricts movement of the legs and feet, and clothing should be loose and comfortable.

Wearing properly fitted graduated compression stockings may be helpful. These compress the calf muscles and improve the flow of blood in the deep veins. They may also help prevent the swollen ankles that are quite common on long flights. However, they need to be the correct size to be effective and passengers should therefore ask their doctor or a travel medicine clinic which type would be appropriate for them.

In view of the clear risk of significant side effects and absence of clear evidence of benefit, passengers are advised not to use aspirin just for the prevention of travel-related DVT.

Those travellers who are at most risk of developing DVT may be prescribed specific treatments, such as injections of heparin. Cabin crew are not trained to give injections and travellers who have been prescribed these must either be taught to give the injections themselves or make other arrangements to have them given by a qualified person.

Diving

Divers should not fly too soon after diving because of the risk that the reduced cabin pressure may lead to decompression sickness (the bends). It is recommended that they do not fly until at least 12 hours after their last dive and this period should be extended to 24 hours after multiple dives or after diving that requires decompression stops during ascent to the surface. Passengers undertaking recreational diving before flying should seek specialist advice from diving schools.

Jet Lag

Jet lag is the term used for the symptoms caused by the disruption of the body's internal clock and the approximate 24-hour (circadian) rhythms it controls. Disruption occurs when crossing multiple time zones i.e. when flying east to west or west to east. Jet lag may lead to indigestion and disturbance of bowel function, general malaise, daytime sleepiness, difficulty in sleeping at night, and reduced physical and mental performance. Its effects are often combined with tiredness due to the journey itself. Jet lag symptoms gradually wear off as the body adapts to the new time zone.

Jet lag cannot be prevented but there are some ways to reduce its effects (see below). Travellers who take medication according to a strict timetable (e.g. insulin, oral contraceptives) should seek medical advice from their doctor or a travel medicine clinic before their journey.

General measures to reduce the effects of jet lag are the following:

— Be as well rested as possible before departure, and rest during the flight. Short naps can be helpful.

— Eat light meals and limit consumption of alcohol. Alcohol increases urine output which can result in disturbed sleep by causing awakenings in order to urinate. Whilst it can accelerate sleep onset, it reduces sleep quality, making sleep less recuperative. The after effects of alcohol (hangover) can exacerbate the effects of jet lag and travel fatigue. Alcohol should therefore be consumed in moderation, if at all, before and during flight. Caffeine should be limited to normal amounts and avoided within a few hours of an anticipated period of sleep.

— Try to create the right conditions when preparing for sleep. When taking a nap during the day, eyeshades and earplugs may help. Regular exercise during the day may help to promote sleep, but avoid strenuous exercise immediately before sleep.

— At the destination, try to get as much sleep in every 24 hours as normal. A minimum block of 4 hours sleep during the local night - known as "anchor sleep" - is thought to be necessary to allow the body's internal clock to adapt to the new time zone. If possible, make up the total sleep time by taking naps at times when feeling sleepy during the day.

— The cycle of light and dark is one of the most important factors in setting the body's internal clock. Exposure to daylight at the destination will usually help adaptation.

— Short-acting sleeping pills may be helpful. They should be used only in accordance with medical advice and should not normally be taken during the flight, as they may increase immobility and therefore the risk of developing DVT.

— Melatonin is available in some countries and can be used to help resynchronize the body's internal clock. It is normally sold as a food supplement and therefore is not subject to the same strict control as medications. The timing and effective dosage of melatonin have not been fully evaluated and its side effects, particularly if used long term, are unknown. In addition, manufacturing methods are not standardised and therefore the dose in each tablet can be very variable and some harmful compounds may be present. For these reasons, melatonin cannot be recommended.

— It is not always appropriate to adjust to local time for short trips of 2-3 days or less. If in doubt, seek specialist travel medicine advice.

— Individuals react in different ways to time zone changes. Frequent flyers should learn how their own body responds and adopt habits accordingly. Advice from a travel medicine clinic may be beneficial in determining an effective coping strategy.

Psychological Aspects

Travel by air is not a natural activity for humans and many people experience some degree of psychological difficulty when flying. The main problems encountered are stress and fear of flying. These may occur together or separately at different times before and during the period of travel.

Stress

All forms of travel generate stress. Flying can be particularly stressful because it often involves a long journey to the airport, curtailed sleep and the need to walk long distances in the terminal building. Most passengers find their own ways of coping, but passengers who find air travel particularly stressful should seek medical advice in good time. Good planning (passports, tickets, medication, etc) and allowing plenty of time to get to the airport helps relieve stress. Flight phobia (fear of flying)

Fear of flying may range from feeling slightly anxious to being unable to travel by air at all. It can lead to problems at work and leisure. Travellers who want to travel by air but are unable to do so because of their fear of flying should seek medical advice before the journey. Medication may be useful in some cases but the use of alcohol "to steady the nerves" is not helpful and may be dangerous if combined with some medicines. For a longer-term solution, travellers should seek specialized treatment to reduce the psychological difficulties associated with air travel. There are many courses available that aim to reduce or cure, fear of flying. These typically include advice on how to cope with the symptoms of fear, information about how an aircraft flies, how controls are operated during a flight and, in most cases, a short flight.

Air rage

In recent years, air rage has been recognized as a form of disruptive behaviour associated with air travel. It appears to be linked to high levels of general stress but not specifically to flight phobia. It is frequently preceded by excessive consumption of alcohol.

Travellers with Medical Conditions

Airlines have the right to refuse to carry passengers with conditions that may worsen, or have serious consequences, during the flight. Airlines may require medical clearance from their medical department/adviser if there is an indication that a passenger could be suffering from any disease or physical or mental condition that:

— May be considered a potential hazard to the safety of the aircraft

— Adversely affects the welfare and comfort of the other passengers and/or crew members

— Requires medical attention and/or special equipment during the flight

— May be aggravated by the flight.

If cabin crew suspect before departure that a passenger may be ill, the aircraft's captain will be informed and a decision taken as to whether the passenger is fit to travel, needs medical attention, or presents a danger to other passengers and crew or to the safety of the aircraft.

Infants

Air travel is not recommended for infants less than seven days old. If travel is absolutely necessary for babies who are over seven days, but were born prematurely, medical advice should be sought in each case. Changes in cabin air pressure may upset infants; this can be helped by feeding or giving a pacifier to stimulate swallowing.

Pregnant women

Pregnant women can normally travel safely by air, but most airlines restrict travel in late pregnancy. Typical guidelines for those who have an uncomplicated pregnancy are:

— after the 28th week of pregnancy a letter from a doctor or midwife should be carried, confirming the expected date of delivery and that the pregnancy is normal

— for single pregnancies, flying is permitted up to the end of the 36th week

— for multiple pregnancies, flying is permitted up to the end of the 32nd week.

Pre-existing illness

Most people with medical conditions are able to travel safely by air, provided that necessary precautions, such as the need for additional oxygen supply, are considered in advance. Those who have underlying health problems such as cancer, heart or lung disease, anaemia, diabetes, are on any form of regular medication or treatment, have recently had surgery or have been in hospital, or who are concerned about their fitness to travel for any other reason, should consult their doctor or a travel medicine clinic before deciding to travel by air.

Medication that may be required during the journey, or soon after arrival, should be carried in the hand luggage. It is also advisable to carry a copy of the prescription in case the medication is lost, additional supplies are needed or security checks require proof of purpose.

Frequent travellers with medical conditions

Frequent travellers who have a permanent and stable underlying health problem may obtain a frequent traveller's medical card from the medical or reservation department of many airlines. This card is accepted, under specified conditions, as proof of medical clearance and for identification of the holder's medical condition.

Security Issues

Security checks can cause concerns for travellers who have been fitted with metal devices such as artificial joints, pacemakers or internal automatic defibrillators. Some pacemakers may be affected by modern security screening equipment and travellers with these should carry a letter from their doctor. Travellers who need to carry other medical equipment in their hand luggage, particularly sharp items such as hypodermic needles, should also carry a letter from their doctor.

Smokers

Almost all airlines now ban smoking on board. Some smokers may find this stressful, particularly during long flights, and should discuss this with their doctor before travelling. Nicotine replacement patches or chewing gum containing nicotine may be helpful during the flight and the use of other medication or techniques may also be considered.

Travellers with Disabilities

A physical disability is not usually a contraindication for travel. Passengers who are unable to look after their own needs during the flight (including use of the toilet and transfer from wheelchair to seat and vice versa) will need to be accompanied by an escort able to provide all necessary assistance. The cabin crew are generally not permitted to provide such assistance and a traveller who requires it and does not have a suitable escort may not be permitted to travel. Travellers confined to wheelchairs should be advised against deliberately restricting their fluid intake before or during travel as a means of avoiding use of toilets during flights as this might detrimentally affect their general health. Airlines have regulations on conditions of travel for passengers with disabilities. Disabled passengers should contact the airline in advance of their travel for guidance.

Communicable Diseases

Research has shown that there is very little risk of any infectious disease being transmitted on board the aircraft. The quality of aircraft cabin air is carefully controlled.

Ventilation rates provide a total change of air 20-30 times per hour. Most modern aircraft have recirculation systems, which recycle up to 50% of cabin air. The recirculated air is usually passed through HEPA (high-efficiency particulate air) filters, of the type used in hospital operating theatres and intensive care units, which trap particles, bacteria, fungi and viruses.

Transmission of infection may occur between passengers who are seated in the same area of an aircraft, usually as a result of the infected person coughing or sneezing or by touch (direct contact or contact with the same parts of the aircraft cabin and furnishings that other passengers touch). This is no different from any other situation where people are close to each other, such as on a train, bus or at a theatre. Highly infectious conditions, such as influenza, are more likely to be spread to other passengers in situations when the aircraft ventilation system is not operating. A small auxiliary power unit is normally used to provide ventilation when the aircraft is on the ground, before the main engines are started, but occasionally this is not operated for environmental (noise) or technical reasons. In such cases, when associated with a prolonged delay, passengers may be temporarily disembarked.

In order to minimise the risk of passing on infections, passengers who are unwell, particularly if they have a fever, should delay their journey until they have recovered. Airlines may deny boarding to passengers who appear to be infected with a communicable disease.

Aircraft Disinsection

Many countries require disinsection of aircraft (to kill insects) arriving from countries where diseases that are spread by insects, such as malaria and yellow fever, occur. There have been a number of cases of malaria affecting individuals who live or work in the vicinity of airports in countries where malaria is not present, thought to be due to the escape of malaria-carrying mosquitoes transported on aircraft. Some countries, e.g. Australia and New Zealand, routinely require disinsection be carried out in order to prevent inadvertent introduction of species that may harm their agriculture.

Disinsection is a public health measure that is mandated by the current International Health Regulations (see Annex 3). It involves treatment of the interior of the aircraft with insecticides specified by WHO. The different procedures currently in use are as follows:

— treatment of the interior of the aircraft using a quick-acting insecticide spray immediately before take-off, with the passengers on board;

— treatment of the interior of the aircraft on the ground before passengers come on board, using a residual insecticide aerosol, plus additional inflight treatment with a quick-acting spray shortly before landing;

— regular application of a residual insecticide to all internal surfaces of the aircraft, except those in food preparation areas.

Travellers are sometimes concerned about their exposure to insecticide sprays while travelling by air. Some people have reported that they feel unwell after spraying of aircraft for disinsection. However, WHO has found no evidence that the specified insecticide sprays are harmful to human health when used as prescribed.

Medical Assistance

Airlines are required to provide minimum levels of medical equipment on aircraft and to train all cabin crew in first aid. The equipment carried varies, with many airlines carrying more than the minimum level of equipment required by the regulations. Equipment carried on a typical international flight would include:

— one or more first-aid kits, to be used by the crew;

— a medical kit, normally to be used by a doctor or other qualified person, to treat in-flight medical emergencies;

— an automated external defibrillator (AED) to be used by the crew in case of cardiac arrest.

Cabin crew are trained in the use of first-aid equipment and in carrying out first-aid and resuscitation procedures. They are usually also trained to recognize a range of medical conditions that may cause emergencies on board and to act appropriately to manage these.

In addition, many airlines have facilities to enable crew to contact a medical expert at a ground-based response centre for advice on how to manage in-flight medical emergencies.

Travel by air is normally contraindicated in the following cases:

— Infants less than 7 days old;

— Women after the 36th week of pregnancy (after 32nd week for multiple pregnancies) and until seven days after delivery;

— Those suffering from:

   — angina pectoris or chest pain at rest

   — any serious or acute infectious disease

   — decompression sickness after diving

   — increased intracranial pressure due to haemorrhage, trauma or infection

   — infections of the sinuses or infections of the ear and nose, particularly if the Eustachian tube is blocked

— recent myocardial infarction and stroke
— recent surgery or injury where trapped air or gas may be present, especially abdominal trauma and gastrointestinal surgery, cranio-facial and ocular injuries, brain operations, and eye operations involving penetration of the eyeball
— severe chronic respiratory disease, breathlessness at rest, or unresolved pneumothorax
— sickle-cell disease
— psychotic illness, except when fully controlled.

The above list is not comprehensive and fitness for travel should be decided on a case-by-case basis.

SECURING YOURSELF

After you've made your reservations, it's time to start preparing for the flight itself. What used to be a quick and easy check-in procedure has evolved into a long and involved trial; fortunately, there are some things you can do to minimize the inevitable annoyances of the post-9/11 era airport check-in.

The first step in minimizing check-in hassle is knowing how to pack. Not in terms of cramming as much stuff as possible into a smallish bag, but rather in managing your possessions to best navigate the airport's multiple security checkpoints. You goals for packing-and dressing-for airline security are to get through the security checkpoints as quickly as possible. You do this by avoiding having your baggage and body searched, and avoiding having your possessions confiscated or disturbed.

Tips for Carry-On Baggage

Here are some tips on what you should and shouldn't pack in your carry-on bags:

— Remove all prohibited items-such as pocket knives, scissors, and tools-from your carry-on baggage.

— Screen your bags before you travel; you may have forgotten a pocket knife or similar item stuck in the back flap six months ago.

— Do not carry-on wrapped gifts; the security screeners will have to unwrap them to examine them.

— Bring the right size carry-on bag

Tips for Dressing for a Date with a Metal Detector

For the most part, items with a small amount of metal-such as rings and bras-will not set off the X-ray machine. However, some machines are more sensitive than others. Consult the following tips to make sure that you pass through without setting off the alarm.

— Remove all jewelry and barrettes.

— Don't wear shoes with steel tips, heels, or shanks.

— Leave metal buttons, snaps, studs, and underwire bras at home.

— Choose watches and belt buckles with a minimal amount of metal.

— Remove any questionable items before you hit the metal detector, and place them in your carry-on luggage.

Tips for Packing Checked Baggage

Keep these tips in mind when packing your big bags:

— Don't lock your bag.

— Avoid creating dense areas in your baggage.

— Don't pack food and beverages inside a checked bag.

— Spread books out; don't stack them.

- Pack in a way that a busy screener can close your bag easily.
- Don't pack what you don't want seen.
- If you don't want it touched, put it in a plastic bag.
- Don't pack wrapped gifts; the screeners will just unwrap them for you.
- Pack shoes, boots, sneakers, and other footwear on top of other contents in your luggage.

More tips for efficient packing:

- X-rays from checked baggage airport scanners will damage unprocessed film. Do not put single-use cameras, rolls of film, or cameras with film still in them in your checked baggage. Conversely, digital camera images or processed film will not be damaged by checked baggage scanners.
- The X-ray equipment used to inspect carry-on baggage will not damage film-so you should carry on all your film. However, if you are going to travel through more than five security checkpoints in a row, request a hand search; the cumulative effect of these low-level x-rays will damage your film. The FAA allows for hand search of photographic film and equipment.
- It is not a good idea to pack your laptop in your checked bags-and certain airlines restrict your doing so. Always carry on your laptop and PDA devices.
- Less is better. If you bring too many bags or overweight/size bags, you could be hit with steep fees. Most problematic are shoes; try to bring one pair that can multitask.

Checking Your Flight Status

It's always good to know if your flight will be leaving or arriving late-or even early. Unfortunately, there are no hard-and-fast rules as to how far in advance you should check this information. Fortunately, there are several Internet-based options for checking the status of a flight.Arrival and departure status is typically available at the airline's Web site, the airport's Web site, and the online travel sites (Expedia, Travelocity, and so on). Each Web site has different features and informational elements; some even offer gate location and wireless and email flight status notification.

Documentation for Domestic Travel

The days of dashing through the security checkpoint and getting your boarding pass at the gate are numbered. In an effort to consolidate passenger screening at the security checkpoints, authorities now requires passengers to present a boarding pass and photo identification at most airports' security checkpoints. Tickets and ticket confirmations (such as a travel agent or airline itineraries) will no. longer be accepted at these checkpoints.

How and Where to Get Your Boarding Pass

Although all these security-related changes might seem daunting, the good news is that airlines have instituted new services that offer more and speedier options for obtaining your boarding pass.

Depending on the airport and. airline, you may be able to obtain your boarding pass at any of these locations:

- — Airport ticket counter
- — Curbside baggage check-in
- — Airport self-service check-in kiosk
- — Over the Internet

Airport Ticket Counter

One thing hasn't changed; you can still get your boarding pass at the airport ticket counter. It's also possible that you won't have to suffer through a long line because most major airlines offer expedited counter service for elite frequent flyer program members and for first and business class travelers.

Curbside Baggage Check-In

Here's a secret that most hardened business travelers know-even with today's heightened security procedures, you can still check your baggage and receive your boarding pass at curbside check-in. Even though it will cost you a small gratuity, this is often the best way to bypass long lines at the ticket counter.

Although most airlines offer curbside check-in at major airports, don't count on this service at smaller airports and with smaller airlines. In addition, government security warnings sometimes force larger airports to limit curbside check-in service.

Airport Self-Service Check-In

This is a new type of check-in, typically available for e-ticket passengers on domestic flights. You will find these self-service kiosks near the ticket counters of most major airlines. The kiosks are touch-screen terminals that display fairly straightforward instructions. To use a self-service check-in terminal, you need a major credit card or frequent flyer card for identification purposes. After you use your card to log in, you can typically obtain boarding passes and seat assignments, check baggage, change flights or standby status, find out about delays or cancellations, and request upgrades. Airlines are rapidly rolling out this self-service check-in at most major airports, but check your airline's Web site to see whether it is available at your airport.

Online Check-in

If you have an e-ticket, are traveling within the United States, and don't need to check baggage, you can print your boarding pass and check in from the comfort of your own home-using your computer and the airline's Web site. This new service lets you print your boarding pass at home or at the office, bring it to the airport, and then head directly to the security checkpoint-no stop at the ticket counter required. To use this service, most airlines require you to be a member of their frequent flyer program, so you should have your frequent flyer number and password or PIN handy when you go online.

E-Tickets

In case you haven't noticed, paper tickets are going the way of the buggy whip. Issuing paper tickets is expensive for airlines, so they're encouraging the use of electronic tickets (e-tickets) instead. You'll find all sorts of incentives to use e-tickets, as well as disincentives to use paper tickets.

Most airlines now charge-considerably-to print a paper ticket. For the traveler, the primary advantage of paper tickets has been that they can be redeemed at other airlines' counters, whereas e-tickets needed to be converted into paper documents at the ticket counter.

Timing Your Arrival

Most business travelers want to minimize the amount of time they spend at the airport. Needless to say, time is precious; it can be irritating to arrive 1 1/2 hours prior to departure and then find yourself cruising to the gate in just 15 minutes. A little information can be helpful to refine your waiting time-without risking a missed flight. If you are in a city you don't know well, check with a local resident or your cab or car service about when to expect rush hour traffic and how it will affect your travel time. So you've made it through the highway traffic; don't assume that you're home free. In some airports the traffic jams around the terminals are worse than on the highways-particularly during the heavy traffic periods or at airports under construction.

The location of your terminal relative to the airport entrance can also add precious minutes to your commute. For example, if you are flying out of LAX during peak travel periods or during major holidays, it can take 10 to 20 minutes to drive from the airport entrance to the farthest terminal.

If you're returning a rental car, take into consideration the location of your rental company drop-off location, whether you can walk or need to take a shuttle to the terminal, and whether the rental car company provides express return service.

It's another issue if you're driving yourself to the airport and need a place to park. If you're a local you probably have a good idea of where to park and know whether you should opt for short-term, long-term, park-and-ride, or economy lots. Check out the airport's Web site to find a map of parking locations and list of rates. Some airport Web sites provide parking availability information, which can save you time trolling for spots.

Also check the airport's Web site for information about parking lots that are closed for security reasons, and to see whether the airport has instituted mandatory vehicle inspection (and how much time you can expect this to take). Now you're inside the terminal. This is when the clock starts ticking for the notorious "recommended arrival time," which is meant to encourage you to leave enough time to get through check-in and security and to your gate prior to the required minimum gate check-in time. Most airlines and airports will tell you to arrive 1 hour prior to departure for domestic flights, or 1 1/2 hours prior if you're checking baggage. If you are traveling during "peak travel" times, you may be told to arrive 1 1/2 to 2 hours prior to departure.

If you are checking bags, some airlines at certain airports require a minimum baggage check-in time to guarantee that your bags will make it on the flight. For example, in Phoenix you need to check bags 30 minutes prior to departure.

Getting Through Security

The airlines authorities has a stated goal of no more than a 10-minute wait time at any of its security checkpoints. The good news is, they're doing a good job of achieving this goal; the days of interminable security lines are, for the most part, long past. If you're concerned about long security lines, you may find wait time information on the airport's Web site. For Some airlines at some airports provide expedited security lanes for certain classes of passengers.

If you think you might want to cut it close, take a look at the airport terminal map (available online at most airport Web sites) and plot your route appropriately. For the airports covered in this book, we have provided information on transportation options and walking times. For example, Atlanta's Hartsfield airport has one central security checkpoint area in the main terminal. If your flight is on Northwest Airlines out of terminal D, you have at most a 2-minute wait for the train and a 5-minute ride (or 15 to 20 minute walk). From there, you'll need only a few extra minutes to get to your gate.

Just because you arrive at the gate with minutes to spare doesn't mean that all is well. You may have missed the minimum gate check-in time required by the airlines-which means you may have lost your seat assignment, or even your seat. (No flight for you!) Although it is rare to find an airline enforcing these requirements.

To retain your preassigned seat assignment, your right to compensation in the case of involuntary denied boarding, and your reservation, airlines require that you check in and be present at the gate by a stated minimum time. This minimum gate arrival time (for domestic flights) ranges from 10 to 30 minutes, with most airlines falling into the 15 to 20 minute range. For example, American West wants you there 20 minutes early, whereas American states a 30-minute minimum.

The problem with determining when you need to check in is that the airlines make this information hard to find. You'll need to examine the fine print on your ticket jacket, or maybe even call the airlines and ask.

Airport Security

Successful navigation of airport security is all about preparing before you get to the airport, as you first learned in the "Packing and Dressing for Airline Security" section. The airlines authority has compiled an extensive list of items permitted and prohibited in both checked and carry-on luggage.

Most airports require a boarding pass and a government-issued photo ID to clear security. If you don't have a boarding pass, you can use a ticket or ticket confirmation, such as a printed itinerary. The challenge is to get through the checkpoint as efficiently as possible and to avoid undergoing a secondary screening. Be aware that any metal detected at the checkpoint must be identified. If you set off the alarm, you will be required to undergo a secondary screening, including a hand-wanding and pat-down inspection.

The airlines authority has created the pithy "IN - OUT - OFF" guideline to help you remember some basic tasks:

— Place all metal items IN your carry-on baggage before you reach the front of the line.

— Take your computer OUT of its carrying case and place it all by itself in one of the bins provided. Make sure that your batteries are working because you may need to turn it on.

— Take OFF your outer coat or jacket so that it can go through the X-ray machine.

Here are some other tips for dealing with airport security:

— Before you get to the checkpoint, remove all jewelry and metal items from your person and place them in your carry-on bag or in one convenient location on your person. Nothing is more irritating than standing behind someone who is pulling PDAs, keys, change, glasses, and so on out of his coat like rabbits out of a hat.

— Wear slip-on shoes. It's much easier to deal with slip-ons than tie-ups if you get chosen for a random screening. In addition, some security screeners require you to place your shoes on the checkpoint conveyor belt, so you might as well prepare for it.

— Choose your shoes carefully. One of the most common ways to trigger the metal detector is to have metal shanks in your shoes. If your loafers are loaded, or you think they might be, take them off and put them in the bin on the conveyor belt.

— If you have a medical implant or similar device, it is likely to set off the alarm on the metal detector-so bring evidence verifying your condition.

— You can bring food through the checkpoint, but it must be wrapped. Beverages have to be in a sealable/spillproof paper or polystyrene (Styrofoam) container.

— If you do not take your computer out if its carrying case before sending it through the X-ray machine, it will need to undergo a secondary screening.

A number of issues are associated with traveling with luggage-security concerns; check-in times; lost or stolen items; and a host of restrictions, allowances, and fees. Fortunately, the odds of having your baggage lost are fairly low. In 2002, less than 0.5% of enplaned passengers filed mishandled baggage reports. If your baggage is lost or damaged, or if items are stolen, contact your airline directly.

Restrictions, Allowances, and Fees

Passengers are limited to one carry-on bag plus a personal item such as a purse, briefcase, or laptop computer. The one carry-on bag must fit in an overhead compartment or under the seat. It should not exceed 45-51 linear inches (length + width + height) or weigh more than 40 pounds.

Every airline has a free baggage allowance, which is the maximum number and size of bags you can carry on or check in without additional charge. Depending on the airline, the free baggage allowance permits 2 to 3 checked bags that weigh less than 70 pounds each and do not exceed 62 linear inches.

Excess and oversized baggage fees are charged if you exceed the free baggage allowance. Most airlines will not allow bags weighing more than 100 pounds-although many will allow you to take one sporting goods item, such as skis or golf clubs, for no additional fee.

If you don't like the idea of a security guard rummaging through your panties or expensive computer equipment, want to avoid excess and oversized baggage fees, or don't want to be troubled with baggage check-in period, you can employ a luggage service to pick up your bags from your home or office and deliver them to your destination. Services typically offer next day, 2-day or 3 to 5 day delivery. Rates vary widely and depend on weight and number of items and pickup and delivery locations.

Airport Lounge Clubs

Major airlines have airline lounge clubs. Located at major airports, airline lounge clubs have standard comfort amenities such as complimentary beverages and snacks, newspapers, televisions, copiers and fax machines, and staff that will assist with ticketing and other services. Many also have computers and printers, as well as workstations with phones and dial-up Internet access. A new trend is the availability of Wi-Fi wireless Internet access; American, Delta, and United have all started rolling out this service in their clubs.

Club memberships are typically offered for annual fees with discounts for spouse membership or multiple year commitments. Airlines also offer free club membership or discounted membership to elite frequent flyer members and sometimes allow you to pay for your membership using frequent flyer miles.

If you tend to fly multiple airlines, you might want to think about joining a network of airport VIP lounges, such as that offered by Priority Pass. Priority Pass membership provides access to more than 400 airport lounges worldwide, regardless of airline flown or class of ticket. Members are welcome at all participating lounges, including more than 100 lounges in 46 U.S. airports. Participating airlines include American West, Continental, Delta, Northwest, United, US Airways, as well as a number of independent lounges. Priority Pass is targeted primarily to international travelers and is often used as a complement to an existing airline airport lounge membership program.

Frequent Flyer Programs

A relatively small group of travelers account for a significant portion of air travel. Although these flyers represent only 8% of the total number of passengers flying in a given year, they make up about 40% of the trips. To entice these heavy-spending customers, the airlines have created incentive-based frequent flyer programs. Almost every airline has some sort of frequent flyer program. These programs range from the incomprehensibly complicated to the sublimely simple. At their most basic, these programs award miles or credits based on the amount you fly-or, in some cases, on the amount you spend.

On the Plane

After you board a plane, you start to notice some real differences between airlines. These differences encompass more than just seat configuration-they extend to meal service, in-flight phones, and even airborne Internet access.

Plane etiquette

Before we get into the available on-board services, here are some tips on how to best get through the boarding and deplaning processes:

— Boarding the airplane rear-to-front, as instructed by most airlines, lets everyone leave sooner.

— Don't block the aisle when boarding; if possible, pull into your seat row while taking off your jacket and stowing your baggage in an overhead compartment.

— Don't place your suitcase on another passenger's suit coat in the overhead compartment.

— Stow your carry-on above your seat or in a compartment in front of you, if possible. If you have to put your carry-on in a compartment in an aisle behind, don't swim upstream when deplaning; wait until everyone has left the plane and then retrieve your bag.

— Turn off your computer, cell phone, and wireless PDA when instructed.

— Don't pull or lean on another passengers seat back.

— Don't stick your feet out into the aisle.

— When the plane lands, don't immediately stand up and hover over your seatmate; wait until you see passengers actually departing before getting out of your seat.

Cabin service

Few travelers mourn the demise of the much-maligned complimentary airline meal service. The full airline meal is now more the exception than the rule-so much so that airport restaurants have begun selling meals you can take on-board, and some airlines have taken to selling meals on their flights. At a handful of airports, you can even order a meal online prior to your flight and pick it up at an airport restaurant.

Airlines that offer meal services will also offer special meals, such as bland, fruit plate, gluten-free, kosher, low calorie, seafood, and vegetarian. You need to reserve these meals ahead of time.

The new buy-on-board services give you the option of purchasing. This service is typically offered on flights shorter than 3 to 4 hours where complimentary meal service is not offered.

Airfone services

Airfone offers voice, data, and fax calling to and from equipped aircraft. Calls can be placed at the gate, during takeoff and landing, and while in-flight. Continental, Delta, Midwest, United, United Express, and US Airways offer Airfone Service on most of their flights; Airfones are located on every first class seat and every middle seat on domestic planes.

Airfone is your only option if you need to make a call while airborne. The Federal Communications Commission (FCC) bans the use of cellular phones on aircraft in the belief that wireless transmissions can interfere with the aircraft's electronic equipment. You can, of course, use your cell phone while the plane is at the gate. Looking forward, several companies are working on developing technology that would allow you to use your cell phone in-flight-but don't expect this type of service for several years.

In-flight internet service

Airlines are beginning to introduce on-board Internet and email service. Two service providers are currently offering these services, on different airlines-Connexion and JetConnect, a product of Verizon.

The Connexion service offers full Internet connectivity but is available only on the international carriers Lufthansa German Airlines and British Airways. Japan Airlines and Scandinavian Airlines System (SAS) have announced plans to equip long-range jetliners in their fleets with the service, starting in 2004. Pricing for the Connexion service is estimated to be around $30 per flight, for a single leg of an international flight. Connexion has indicated that it will be rolling out service in the U.S. in the near future.

The Verizon JetConnect service is less robust. It offers instant messaging, one-way text messaging, news, and games for $5.99 per flight. A companion service, JetConnect with Email, adds the capability to send and receive 2 kilobyte emails (including attachments) for $15.98 per flight plus $.10 for each extra kilobyte. The service is not too speedy, with transmission speed at 9.6 kilobits per second. To use the service, you need an email account that uses either a POP-3, Microsoft Outlook, or Lotus Notes protocol.

In-flight electronic devices

Frequent travelers are familiar with airline restrictions regarding the use of personal electronic devices. The concern is that these devices may cause electromagnetic interference with cockpit navigation or communications systems during ground operations and while the aircraft is flying below 10,000 feet. After the aircraft is above 10,000 feet you can use your devices.

Devices that can be used during the flight-but not during takeoff and landing-include calculators, handheld computer games, shavers, portable CD and tape players, videotape and DVD players, PDAs, and laptop computers and accessories. Note that the FAA doesn't specifically ban the use of these personal electronic devices but has stated that the airlines must prove that they do not interfere with flight operations before they allow passengers to use them below 10,000 feet-thus the continuing ban, in the name of safety.

On-board power ports

If you are looking to spend your flight working on your laptop, your best bets are American, Delta, United, and US Airways, all of which offer power ports on select aircraft. These outlets provide 15V direct current to operate laptop computers and CD/DVD players, and to charge cell phones and other devices. Use of power ports is permitted only when the aircraft is above 10,000 feet in altitude and the flight attendant announces that personal electronic devices are allowed.

To use a power port, you'll need a compatible DC auto/air power adapter. These cords can be purchased at most electronics stores, at LapTop Lane outlets, or through power cord manufacturers. Keep in mind that power adapter cords are device and model specific-although you can always go with the IGo Juice power cord, which is an all-in-one power adapter (retail price $119.99) that connects your device to any AC or DC power source. The Juice cord can also simultaneously power mobile phone or handheld devices, along with your notebook.

Seating

If you do any flying at all, you know how uncomfortable the average airplane seat is-in economy class, anyway. You also know that some airline seats are less uncomfortable than others. Let's take a few minutes to examine what makes for a more or less comfortable airplane seat. Not all airline seats are created equal. The difference lies in just a few inches of difference in seat pitch and width.

Seat pitch is the number of inches from any point on a seat to the exact point on the seat in front or behind it. Pitch is an approximate measure of legroom; the greater the seat pitch, the greater the amount of legroom. Seat width, on the other hand, is the measurement from one edge of your seat to the other.

Seat pitch and width vary wildly by airline, by airplane, and (especially) by class of service. The bottom line is that two or three extra inches one way or the other can make a big difference to your personal comfort. And some airlines (such as JetBlue, Midwest, and Song) have bet their bottom line that passengers appreciate the difference.

Another important factor in passenger comfort is seat configuration. The configuration denotes how seats are grouped within a row. For example, a 3-2 configuration means three seats, an aisle, and then two more seats. Configuration helps you determine the odds of being stuck in the notorious middle seat-or, looking on the bright side, of having a possible empty seat between you and your row mate.

First and foremost, ask the reservation agent for the seat you want. Particularly if you have a connecting flight, you will want a seat in the front of the plane. The 10 minutes you wait for other passengers to deplane could cost you your connection. Ask whether there are places on the plane with fewer people if that is important to you. Avoid the last row of the plane where seats don't recline and are noisier. Rebook your seat assignment an hour or so before your flight. Airlines hold back part of their inventory for day of departure assignments; this includes the coveted bulkhead and exit row seats.

ALTERNATIVES TO COMMERCIAL AIR TRAVEL

Charter airline service is an increasingly popular option for business travelers, particularly since commercial carriers have begun to reduce schedules. You may want to consider a charter option if you

— Are flying to a destination not served-or not conveniently served-by commercial airlines
— Require on-demand service
— Are traveling with a group
— Need to travel to multiple destinations
— Want to avoid congestion and security at larger airports

— Can't afford to spend the time it might take using commercial airline options

Your best bet for booking a charter flight is to go through a charter broker. These companies act like travel agents and will find the least-expensive options with the highest-quality charter aircraft services. One such company is Air Charter Team. There are always less expensive ways to travel than charter, but costs continue to drop, thanks to aircraft overcapacity and improved logistics technology that allows brokers to schedule aircraft more efficiently. Pricing for charters depends on a number of factors, making it impossible to give specific rates, but a rough rule of thumb is that a charter will cost about the same amount as a commercial flight for three people flying first class-or six people flying on nonrefundable coach class tickets.

Private-jet memberships-prepaid blocks of travel on small aircraft-are a viable alternative to corporate jet or fractional ownership. Companies selling private-jet memberships include Marquis Jet Partners, Sentient, and Delta AirElite. Pricing structures vary by company, aircraft, and destination, which makes them difficult to compare; know, however, that you'll pay less for a private-jet membership than you would for a corporate jet.

Another option is offered by Indigo, a corporate-jet service that runs flights out of New Jersey's Teterboro airport and New York's Westchester airport to Midway airport in Chicago. Indigo sells individual seats on these flights, and their fares are competitive with full-fare economy class seats on major commercial carriers.

BIBLIOGRAPHY

Adams, Kathleen M., "Come to Tana Toraja, "Land of the Heavenly Kings: Travel Agents as Brokers in Ethnicity", *Annals of Tourism Research*, 1984.

_____., "Distant Encounters: Travel Literature and the Shifting Images of the Toraja of Sulawesi", Indonesia. Terrae Incognitae, 1991.

Baier, S., "The Economic Impact of Travel and Tourism in a Mountain Area: The Case of Vorarlberg, Austria", *In Tourism: The State of the Art*, A. V. Seaton, ed., Chichester, England: Wiley, 1994.

Bechdolt, B. V., "Cross-Sectional Travel Demand Functions: U.S. Visitors to Hawaii", *Quarterly Review of Economics and Business*, Winter, 1973.

Böröcz, József, "Travel-Capitalism: The Structure of Europe and the Advent of the Tourist", *Comparative Studies in Society and History*, 1992.

Buck, Roy C., and Ted Alleman, "Tourist Enterprise Concentration and Old Order Amish Survival: Explorations in Productive Coexistence", *Journal of Travel Research*, 1979.

Caneday, L., and J. Zeiger, "The Social, Economic, and Environmental Costs of Tourism to a Gaming Community as Perceived by Its Residents", *Journal of Travel Research*, 1991.

Casson, Jean, "From Travel to Tourism", *Communications*, 1967.

Chambers, Erve, "Native Tours: The Anthropology of Travel and Tourism", *Prospect Heights*, Illinois: Waveland, 2000.

Dann, Graham M. S., "Travel by Train: Keeping Nostalgia on Track", *In Tourism: The State of the Art*, A. V. Seaton, ed., Chichester, England: Wiley, 1994.

Dervaes, Claudine, *The Travel Dictionary*, Tampa: Solitaire,1992.

Frew, E., "International Charter Travel—a New Opportunity for Australian Tourism", *In Tourism: The State of the Art*, A. V. Seaton, ed. Pp. 178-185. Chichester, England: Wiley, 1994.

Hiller, Herbert L., "Where Is Tourism Traveling?", *Journal of Interamerican Studies and World Affairs*, 1974.

Hudson, Kenneth, "Air Travel: A Social History", Totowa, New Jersey: Rowman and Littlefield, 1972.

INDEX